GoodFood
101 FRUITY PUDS

Published in 2009 by BBC Books,
an imprint of Ebury Publishing
A Random House Group company

Recipes © BBC *Good Food*
magazine 2009
Book design © Woodlands Books Ltd 2009
All photographs © BBC *Good Food*
magazine 2009
All recipes contained within this book first
appeared in BBC *Good Food* magazine

The Random House Group Limited
Reg. No. 954009

Addresses for companies within the
Random House Group can be found at
www.randomhouse.co.uk

A CIP catalogue record for this book is available
from the British Library.

The Random House Group Limited supports
The Forest Stewardship Council (FSC), the
leading international forest certification organization.
All our titles that are printed on Greenpeace
approved FSC certified paper carry the FSC logo.
Our paper procurement policy can be found at
www.rbooks.co.uk/environment

To buy books by your favourite authors and
register for offers visit www.rbooks.co.uk

Printed and bound by Firmengruppe APPL,
aprinta druck, Wemding, Germany
Colour origination by Dot Gradations Ltd, UK

Commissioning Editor: Lorna Russell
Project Editor: Laura Higginson
Designer: Annette Peppis
Production: David Brimble
Picture Researcher: Gabby Harrington

ISBN: 9781846077234

GoodFood

101 FRUITY PUDS
TRIPLE-TESTED RECIPES

Editor
Jane Hornby

Contents

Introduction

Can you imagine June without strawberries and cream, October without apple pie, Christmas without Christmas pudding? Whatever the season, there is a perfect fruit recipe for every occasion and in *101 Fruity Puds* we've collected our best fruity ideas.

Nothing says party more than a special pudding – and we have a great selection of celebration desserts and special fruit cakes, from mallowy meringues to creamy cheesecakes. Everyday puds, on the other hand, need to be quick and easy. That's why we've included plenty of recipes for sweet treats ready, or in the oven, in no time.

Temptation finds more forms in stress-free ices, bombes and sorbets that can be pulled from the freezer. And if it's cold outside you'll find comfort in our winter-warming pies and puddings just waiting for a good dollop of custard or cream.

Whatever you pick, there'll be a nutritional breakdown handy to help you work out exactly how much you feel like spoiling yourself. And, of course, each recipe has been tested by us, to make sure it will work first time for you.

Jane

Jane Hornby
Good Food magazine

Notes and conversion tables

NOTES ON THE RECIPES
• Eggs are large in the UK and Australia and extra large in America unless stated otherwise.
• Wash fresh produce before preparation.
• Recipes contain nutritional analyses for 'sugar', which means the total sugar content including all natural sugars in the ingredients unless otherwise stated.

OVEN TEMPERATURES

Gas	°C	Fan °C	°F	Oven temp.
¼	110	90	225	Very cool
½	120	100	250	Very cool
1	140	120	275	Cool or slow
2	150	130	300	Cool or slow
3	160	140	325	Warm
4	180	160	350	Moderate
5	190	170	375	Moderately hot
6	200	180	400	Fairly hot
7	220	200	425	Hot
8	230	210	450	Very hot
9	240	220	475	Very hot

APPROXIMATE WEIGHT CONVERSIONS
• All the recipes in this book list both imperial and metric measurements. Conversions are approximate and have been rounded up or down. Follow one set of measurements only; do not mix the two.
• Cup measurements, which are used by cooks in Australia and America, have not been listed here as they vary from ingredient to ingredient. Kitchen scales should be used to measure dry/solid ingredients.

Good Food are concerned about sustainable sourcing and animal welfare so where possible, we use organic ingredients, humanely-reared meats, free-range chickens and eggs and unrefined sugar.

SPOON MEASURES

Spoon measurements are level unless otherwise specified.

- 1 teaspoon (tsp) = 5ml
- 1 tablespoon (tbsp) = 15ml
- 1 Australian tablespoon = 20ml (cooks in Australia should measure 3 teaspoons where 1 tablespoon is specified in a recipe)

APPROXIMATE LIQUID CONVERSIONS

metric	imperial	AUS	US
50ml	2fl oz	¼ cup	¼ cup
125ml	4fl oz	½ cup	½ cup
175ml	6fl oz	¾ cup	¾ cup
225ml	8fl oz	1 cup	1 cup
300ml	10fl oz/½ pint	½ pint	1¼ cups
450ml	16fl oz	2 cups	2 cups/1 pint
600ml	20fl oz/1 pint	1 pint	2½ cups
1 litre	35fl oz/1¾ pints	1¾ pints	1 quart

You can rustle up this dish in moments, using a bag of plums and a few storecupboard staples.

Lemon French toast with poached plums

2 eggs, beaten
100ml/3½fl oz milk
zest of 1 lemon
4 tbsp caster sugar
4 slices bread or brioche, cut in half diagonally
50g/2oz butter
450g/1lb plums, halved and stoned
1 tbsp fresh lemon juice
crème fraîche or vanilla ice cream, to serve

Takes 30 minutes • Serves 4

1 Mix the eggs, milk, lemon zest and 1 tablespoon of the sugar in a shallow dish. Add the bread or brioche, then turn in the liquid until well soaked.

2 Put 2 tablespoons of the sugar and half the butter in a frying pan, then heat gently until the sugar has melted. Add the plums, then fry until they are softened and the juice is golden brown, about 5 minutes. Add the lemon juice, then heat gently to make a light syrup.

3 Heat the remaining butter in a large non-stick frying pan, then add the soaked slices of bread or brioche and fry on each side until golden brown. Put two slices on each plate, sprinkle with the remaining sugar, then spoon over the plums and their juice. Serve as they are or with crème fraîche or vanilla ice cream.

• Per serving (without crème fraîche or ice cream)
331 kcalories, protein 8g, carbohydrate 44g, fat 15g, saturated fat 8g, fibre 2g, sugar 28g, salt 0.78g

This light, fresh-tasting dessert looks elegant served in wine glasses with a few amaretti biscuits on the side or topped with a spoonful of mascarpone or good vanilla ice cream.

Cherries in rosé wine and vanilla syrup

425ml/¾ pint rosé wine
1 vanilla pod, split lengthways
100g/4oz demerara sugar
500g/1lb 2oz cherries

Takes 30 minutes • Serves 4
(easily doubled)

1 Tip the wine into a medium pan, then add the vanilla pod with the sugar. Bring to the boil, then reduce the heat and simmer until the sugar has dissolved.
2 Stone the cherries, if you like, or leave them as they are. Add to the pan and cook gently for 6 minutes. Remove the cherries with a slotted spoon to a bowl. Set aside.
3 Increase the heat, then boil the remaining liquid for 8–10 minutes until slightly syrupy. Pour over the cherries then divide the fruit and the syrup among four glass bowls. Serve warm or cold with a few amaretti biscuits.

• Per serving 199 kcalories, protein 1g, carbohydrate 43g, fat none, saturated fat none, fibre 1g, sugar 43g, salt 0.02g

The classic Eton Mess is made with meringue that takes about an hour to make. These meringues take seconds to make and then, using a microwave, just a few seconds more to cook.

Eton Mess stacks

1 egg white
350g/12oz icing sugar, plus extra
for dusting
1 tsp crushed cardamom seeds
(optional)
a little oil, for greasing
142ml pot double cream
juice of ½ lemon
250g punnet raspberries

Takes 20 minutes • Serves 4

1 Lightly whisk the egg white, then sift in the icing sugar and cardamom to make a firm fondant icing. Roll into eight golfball-sized balls (you probably won't need all of it). Two at a time, put the balls at opposite ends of a greased piece of non-stick baking paper, then microwave for 30–40 seconds on High until quadrupled in size. Leave to cool for a few minutes, then lift off the paper and repeat until all the balls are cooked.

2 Whip the cream with the lemon juice. Crush half the raspberries, then fold through the cream. To serve, put a little splodge of raspberry cream on to four plates. Stack a meringue with some more cream, then place another meringue on top. Spoon over more cream, then top with a few whole raspberries. Dust with icing sugar and serve.

• Per serving 550 kcalories, protein 2g, carbohydrate 96g, fat 20g, saturated fat 11g, fibre 2g, sugar 94g, salt 0.10g

It takes just a couple of minutes to prepare this warming family pudding, made from handy frozen fruit.

Berry slump

100g/4oz butter, softened, plus extra for greasing
100g/4oz caster sugar, plus 2 tbsp extra
100g/4oz self-raising flour
2 eggs
1 tbsp milk
2 tsp vanilla extract
600g/1lb 5oz frozen mixed summer berries
25g/1oz flaked almonds
custard or vanilla ice cream, to serve

Takes 50 minutes • Serves 4–6

1 Preheat the oven to 180°C/fan 160°C/gas 4. In a food processor, whiz together the butter, 100g of sugar, flour, eggs, milk and 1 teaspoon of the vanilla extract until smooth.
2 Lightly grease a medium baking dish, then tip in the frozen fruit. Scatter over the remaining sugar and vanilla extract. Dollop over the cake mix, then smooth all over with the back of a spoon to cover the fruit. Make a little dip in the middle of the mixture to ensure it cooks evenly throughout. Scatter over the almonds.
3 Put in the oven and cook for 45 minutes until the fruit is hot and the sponge is cooked through. Serve warm with custard or vanilla ice cream.

• Per serving (4) 530 kcalories, protein 9g, carbohydrate 64g, fat 28g, saturated fat 14g, fibre 5g, sugar 46g, salt 0.78g

Bring out the scented flavour of ripe peaches with
a quick-and-easy honey sauce.

Honeyed fruit sundaes

50g/2oz butter
1 vanilla pod, seeds scraped out
3 tbsp runny honey
200g punnet blueberries
2 or 3 ripe peaches, cut into wedges
8 Belgian waffle biscuits
real vanilla ice cream

Takes 12 minutes • Serves 4

1 Heat a frying pan, then add the butter.
Once it foams, add the vanilla seeds and
honey. Stir in the blueberries and peach
wedges, then gently warm through to release
the syrupy juices. (Don't boil them or the
peach flesh will turn fluffy.)
2 Put a couple of waffle biscuits on to four
plates, half overlapping. Top with some of the
fruit and spoonfuls of the syrup, then add a
scoop of ice cream.

• Per serving 411 kcalories, protein 5g, carbohydrate
48g, fat 24g, saturated fat 14g, fibre 2g, sugar 35g,
salt 0.46g

Thick and fluffy pancakes go fantastically with sticky apples. You can make them ahead of time then warm them through in the microwave or an oven set at a low heat. Serve with vanilla ice cream.

Butterscotch apple pancakes

FOR THE PANCAKES
200g/8oz self-raising flour
1 egg, beaten
200ml/7fl oz milk
sunflower or vegetable oil, for frying

FOR THE APPLES
250g/9oz soft brown sugar
100g/4oz unsalted butter
splash of fresh lemon juice or brandy
4 large Bramley apples, peeled and
each cut into eight

Takes 20 minutes • Serves 4

1 To make the apples, tip the sugar and butter into a pan, and melt over a low heat. Stir and bubble for about 5 minutes. Add the lemon juice or brandy and the apples. Cook for about 7 minutes until the apples are softened.
2 Meanwhile, put the flour into a large bowl, add a pinch of salt, then make a well in the centre of the flour. Add the egg and a splash of the milk, beat until smooth, then add the rest of the milk to make a batter.
3 Heat a large non-stick frying pan, then add a splash of oil. Pour four small pools of batter into the pan, well spaced apart, and leave for 1 minute or until the surface starts to bubble. Flip over and fry for 30 seconds until golden and puffed. Slide on to baking parchment, cover and keep warm. Repeat with the remaining batter. When all the pancakes are made, serve with the apples and butterscotch sauce.

• Per serving 698 kcalories, protein 9g, carbohydrate 114g, fat 27g, saturated fat 14g, fibre 3g, sugar 76g, salt 0.62g

These quick puds combine two raspberry classics and can be made a couple of hours ahead and kept in the fridge.

Summer pudding trifles

600g/1lb 5oz raspberries
50g/2oz golden caster sugar
1 Madeira cake (about 300g/10oz)
227ml pot clotted cream
icing sugar, to dust

Takes 20 minutes • Serves 4

1 Set aside half the raspberries. In a bowl, roughly mash the remaining raspberries with the sugar. Set aside.

2 Cut the Madeira loaf into 12 slices, then use a round cutter to cut out 12 rounds of the cake to fit four serving glasses.

3 Layer up the trifles in glasses starting with a slice of cake, then some cream and some mashed raspberries. After the final slice of cake, spread over some cream and top with the whole raspberries. The trifles can be kept in the fridge for a couple of hours. Dust with a little icing sugar before serving.

• Per serving 617 kcalories, protein 6g, carbohydrate 53g, fat 44g, saturated fat 27g, fibre 4g, sugar 42g, salt 0.52g

If you're making this for children as well as adults, mix the juice from the orange with the strawberries and sugar, then splash a little Cointreau over the adult portions when you serve.

Zesty strawberries with Cointreau

500g/1lb 2oz strawberries, hulled and halved or quartered, depending on size
3 tbsp Cointreau
zest of 1 orange
4 tbsp icing sugar
mint leaves, roughly torn, to serve

Takes about 5 minutes, plus 1 hour marinating • Serves 4

1 Tip the strawberries into a large bowl. Splash over the Cointreau, add the orange zest and sift in the icing sugar, then give everything a really good mix. Cover, then leave for 1 hour or more for the juices to become syrupy and the strawberries to soak up some of the alcohol.
2 To serve, scatter the mint leaves over the strawberries and give them one more good stir, then spoon into four individual glass dishes.

• Per serving 69 kcalories, protein 1g, carbohydrate 10g, fat none, saturated fat none, fibre 1g, sugar 10g, salt 0.02g

This compote is delicious served either warm with ice cream,
or cold for breakfast with yogurt.

Roasted stone fruits with vanilla

175g/6oz golden caster sugar
1 vanilla pod, split in two
5 cardamom pods
zest and juice of 1 lime
6 apricots, halved and stoned
3 peaches, quartered and stoned
3 nectarines, quartered and stoned
ice cream, to serve

Takes 30 minutes • Serves 4

1 Preheat oven to 220°C/fan 200°C/gas 7.
Tip the sugar, vanilla pod, cardamom, lime
zest and juice into a food processor, then
blitz until blended, or mash together using a
pestle and mortar. Tip the fruit into a shallow
baking dish, then toss in the sludgy sugar.
2 Roast for 20 minutes until the fruits have
softened but not collapsed and the sugar and
fruit juices have made a sticky sauce. Leave
the fruit to cool a little, then serve straight
from the dish with ice cream.

• Per serving 270 kcalories, protein 3g, carbohydrate
68g, fat none, saturated fat none, fibre 4g, sugar 68g,
salt 0.02g

Syllabubs taste really special and look impressive served with a few berries and thin biscuits, but they take just minutes to make.

Lemon syllabub

284ml pot whipping cream
50g/2oz caster sugar
50ml/2fl oz white wine
zest and juice of ½ lemon
almond thins or fresh berries,
to serve

Takes 10 minutes • Serves 4

1 Whip together the cream and sugar until soft peaks form. Stir in the wine, most of the lemon zest and the juice. Spoon the syllabub into four glasses or bowls, sprinkle with the remaining zest and serve with almond thins or berries.

• Per serving 328 kcalories, protein 2g, carbohydrate 15g, fat 29g, saturated fat 18g, fibre none, sugar 15g, salt 0.05g

Home-made rice pudding is simple to make, but if you haven't time then use a good-quality ready-made one instead. A few strawberries added to the rhubarb bring out its flavour and colour.

Rhubarb rice pots

85g/3oz short grain rice
50g/2oz caster sugar, plus 3 tbsp
600ml/1 pint milk
1 vanilla pod, split
142ml pot whipping or double cream
300g/10oz rhubarb, cut into
2cm chunks
3–4 strawberries, hulled and halved
(optional)

Takes 45 minutes, plus chilling
Serves 4

1 Put the rice, 50g caster sugar, the milk and vanilla pod in a pan, then slowly bring to the boil. Reduce the heat, partially cover, then simmer for 30 minutes, stirring occasionally until the rice is tender. Make sure you keep the heat low and the pan partially covered to avoid the milk boiling over. Tip the mixture into a bowl, then leave to cool. Remove the vanilla pod.

2 Whip the cream until it just holds its shape, then fold into the rice. Cover and chill until ready to serve.

3 Put the rhubarb in a pan with the remaining sugar, 1 tablespoon of water and the strawberries, if using. Gently heat, then cover and cook until the rhubarb is tender. Leave to cool.

4 To serve, spoon the rice into four dishes or glasses and then spoon over the rhubarb.

• Per serving 389 kcalories, protein 8g, carbohydrate 53g, fat 17g, saturated fat 10g, fibre 1g, sugar 38g, salt 0.20g

You'll never buy a sponge pud again once you've made this tangy dessert that's ready in 10 minutes.

Fastest-ever lemon pudding

100g/4oz golden caster sugar
100g/4oz softened butter
100g/4oz self-raising flour
2 eggs
zest of 1 lemon
1 tsp vanilla extract
4 tbsp lemon curd
crème fraîche or ice cream, to serve

Takes 10 minutes • Serves 4

1 Beat together the sugar, butter, flour, eggs, lemon zest and vanilla extract until creamy, then spoon into a medium-sized microwave-proof baking dish. Microwave on High for 3 minutes, turning the dish around halfway through cooking, until the sponge is evenly risen and cooked set all the way through. Leave to stand for 1 minute.
2 Meanwhile, heat the lemon curd for 30 seconds in the microwave and stir until smooth. Pour all over the top of the pudding and serve with a dollop of crème fraîche or scoops of ice cream.

• Per serving 457 kcalories, protein 6g, carbohydrate 55g, fat 25g, saturated fat 14g, fibre 1g, sugar 34g, salt 0.75g

Bring a taste of summer to a winter's day with this tasty berry pud.

White chocolate and berry pudding

100g/4oz butter, softened, plus extra
for greasing
100g/4oz light brown soft sugar
100g/4oz self-raising flour
2 eggs
3 tbsp milk
85g/3oz white chocolate drops
300g pack frozen mixed berries
icing sugar, for dusting
custard, to serve

Takes 25 minutes • Serves 4

1 Preheat oven to 180°C/fan 160°C/gas 4. Lightly butter a medium baking dish. Beat together the butter, sugar, flour, eggs and milk with an electric hand whisk until light and fluffy.
2 Fold through the white chocolate and most of the berries, pour into the dish, then bake for 20 minutes until risen and golden. Warm the remaining berries a little in a pan or in the microwave. Dust the top of the pudding with icing sugar and serve with the warm berries and some custard.

• Per serving 550 kcalories, protein 9g, carbohydrate 63g, fat 31g, saturated fat 18g, fibre 3g, sugar 44g, salt 0.83g

Little caramel banana tarts make a great alternative to jelly
and ice cream for a child's birthday-party pudding.

Banoffee bites

1 tbsp caster sugar
a good pinch of ground cinnamon
225g pack frozen ready-rolled shortcrust pastry, defrosted
284ml pot double cream
2 medium bananas, peeled and chopped
3 tbsp Dulce de Leche Caramel sauce (available from Merchant Gourmet)
50g/2oz toffee-coated popcorn

Takes 30 minutes, plus chilling
Makes 12

1 Mix together the sugar and cinnamon. Sprinkle a work surface with half of the cinnamon mixture, unroll the pastry on to it and scatter with the rest. Lightly roll out the pastry a little more so that the cinnamon sugar is pressed into the dough. Using a 7cm cutter, cut out 12 rounds and use to line a greased 12-hole bun tin, re-rolling any trimmings if you need to. With a fork, prick the bottom of each pastry case. Set aside to chill for 20 minutes. Preheat oven to 190°C/fan 170°C/gas 5.
2 Meanwhile, make the filling: whip the cream until it forms soft peaks, then gently stir in the bananas and caramel sauce.
3 Bake the pastry cases for 8–10 minutes until light golden and crisp. Cool, then remove to a plate. Spoon the banana mixture into the cases and top with the popcorn. Serve straight away.

• Per bite 254 kcalories, protein 2g, carbohydrate 20g, fat 19g, saturated fat 9g, fibre 1g, sugar 10g, salt 0.22g

Adding ricotta to thick American-style pancakes gives them a delicious light creaminess that goes perfectly with the blueberries – heaven with a good drizzle of syrup!

Blueberry and ricotta pancakes

250g/9oz ricotta
175ml/6fl oz milk
4 eggs, separated
100g/4oz plain flour
1 tsp baking powder
4 tbsp golden caster sugar
150g punnet blueberries
butter, for frying
maple syrup and vanilla ice cream, to serve

Takes 20 minutes • Makes about 14 pancakes

1 Place the ricotta, milk and egg yolks in a large bowl, and beat well with a pinch of salt. Sift the flour and baking powder into the mixture, then add the sugar and stir to a smooth batter. In a separate bowl, use an electric whisk to beat the egg whites until stiff. Carefully fold into the batter, then fold in the blueberries.
2 Heat a little butter in a large non-stick frying pan and drop small ladlefuls of the mixture, well spaced apart, into the pan. Cook in batches for 1 minute on each side until puffed up and golden. Pile the pancakes on to serving plates, drizzle over maple syrup and top with a scoop of ice cream.

• Per pancake 121 kcalories, protein 5g, carbohydrate 12g, fat 6g, saturated fat 3g, fibre none, sugar 6g, salt 0.27g

Ambrosia is traditionally served as part of the Thanksgiving meal in America. It is the perfect dessert to follow a rich main course, and the fruits used are all really good in the autumn.

Ambrosia

4 oranges
1 tbsp clear honey or light muscovado sugar
small bunch of seedless black or red grapes
300g/10oz fresh pineapple chunks
chunk of fresh coconut or a handful of flaked coconut
a handful of pecan nut halves

Takes 15 minutes • Serves 4–6

1 Finely grate the zest from one orange into a bowl and squeeze out its juice. Add the honey or sugar to the zest and juice, and mix well. Pare the zest and pith from the remaining oranges and cut down between the membranes to separate the segments. Do this over the bowl to catch the juice.
2 Halve the grapes, if necessary. Add the grapes and pineapple to the orange segments and juice.
3 If using fresh coconut, shave into thin slices with a potato peeler. Stir the coconut into the fruit salad, then cover and chill until ready to serve, up to 24 hours ahead. Sprinkle with the pecans before serving.

• Per serving (4) 218 kcalories, protein 3g, carbohydrate 35g, fat 8g, saturated fat 2g, fibre 5g, sugar 35g, salt 0.03g

Making your own jelly by using a good-quality smoothie means a lot more flavour and a lot less sugar.

Smoothie jellies with ice cream

6 sheets leaf gelatine
1 litre bottle orange, mango and passion fruit smoothie
500ml tub good-quality vanilla ice cream, to serve

Takes 5 minutes, plus setting time
Makes 12 small or 24 mini pots

1 Put the leaf gelatine in a bowl and cover with cold water. Leave for a few minutes until soft and floppy. Meanwhile, gently heat the smoothie in a pan without boiling. Take off the heat.
2 Lift the gelatine out of the water, squeeze out the excess water, then add it to the smoothie pan. Stir well until smooth, then pour into 12 moulds, pots or glasses, or use 24 shot-glass-sized pots. Chill for at least 1 hour to set. Serve each smoothie jelly topped with ice cream.

• Per serving (12 jellies with 1 tbsp ice cream)
92 kcalories, protein 4g, carbohydrate 15g, fat 2g, saturated fat 1g, fibre 2g, sugar 13g, salt 0.05g

Kids will love this healthy tropical pud that's bursting with fruit. Choose kiwis that smell sweet and feel plump, avoiding any with bruised skin. Ripe kiwis should yield very slightly when pressed.

Fruity coconut creams

1 × 50g sachet coconut cream
500g pot 0% fat Greek yogurt or Quark
85g/3oz icing sugar, sieved
a few drops of vanilla extract
2 kiwi fruit
400g can pineapple chunks

Takes 15 minutes • Serves 4

1 Dissolve the coconut cream in 50ml boiling water, then leave to cool. Spoon the yogurt or Quark into a mixing bowl, then stir in the icing sugar and vanilla extract. Combine with the coconut mix, then spoon into four individual glasses. Chill until ready to serve.
2 Peel and chop the kiwi fruit into small pieces. Drain the pineapple, then chop the chunks into small pieces. Mix together the fruit, then spoon over the top of the coconut creams to serve.

• Per serving 266 kcalories, protein 19g, carbohydrate 40g, fat 5g, saturated fat 4g, fibre 1g, sugar 39g, salt 0.16g

This has to be the simplest dessert ever. Plonk a plate of ripe strawberries and honeyed ricotta in the middle of the table, and let everyone dig in.

Honey-nut ricotta with strawberries

200g/8oz ricotta
2 tbsp clear honey, to taste
a handful of toasted almonds
400g strawberries, halved

Takes 2 minutes • Serves 4

1 Tip the ricotta out on to a large serving plate and drizzle with honey.
2 Sprinkle over the almonds and spread the strawberries around the plate. Serve with spoons for everyone to dig in.

• Per serving 159 kcalories, protein 7g, carbohydrate 13g, fat 9g, saturated fat 4g, fibre 2g, sugar 13g, salt 0.15g

Bananas and custard meet bread and butter pudding.
Serve with a little cream or a drizzle of toffee sauce.

Banana bread and butter pudding

4 thick slices white bread
50g/2oz butter, softened
1 large banana, peeled and sliced
1 tbsp cornflour
450ml/16fl oz milk
2 eggs
85g/3oz soft light brown sugar, plus
1 tbsp extra
a large pinch of ground cinnamon

Takes 20 minutes • Serves 4

1 Toast the bread, spread with the butter and cut each slice into six equal pieces. Arrange, butter-side up, with the banana in a microwave-proof baking dish (approx. 23cm wide by 5cm deep).
2 In a small bowl, mix the cornflour with a little of the milk until smooth. Beat together the eggs, 85g of sugar, cinnamon and remaining milk in a jug then stir in the cornflour. Pour over the bread and banana, then sprinkle with the extra sugar.
3 Cook in the microwave on High for 8–10 minutes. Stand for 5 minutes before serving. If you don't have a microwave, assemble the dish without toasting the bread beforehand then bake at 180°C/fan 160°C/gas 4 for 30 minutes until set.

• Per serving 412 kcalories, protein 10g, carbohydrate 64g, fat 15g, saturated fat 8g, fibre 1g, sugar 38g, salt 0.99g

Frozen raspberries are ideal for this recipe as the juice they release when they thaw adds to the sauciness of the pudding's bottom layer.

Chocolate and raspberry creams

300g/10oz frozen raspberries
1 tbsp brandy (optional)
3 tbsp raspberry conserve
175g/6oz plain chocolate, plus extra grated, to decorate
2 × 150g pots thick and creamy raspberry yogurt
300ml/½ pint fresh vanilla custard

Takes 20 minutes • Serves 6

1 Mix the raspberries with the brandy, if using, and raspberry conserve, then spoon into the bottom of six glasses.
2 Break the chocolate into a microwave-proof bowl, then melt in the microwave on High for 1–2 minutes, or place the bowl over a pan of simmering water and stir until melted.
3 Stir the yogurt and custard into the melted chocolate, then spoon on top of the berries. Cover and chill until ready to serve, then top with grated plain chocolate.

• Per serving 300 kcalories, protein 5g, carbohydrate 43g, fat 13g, saturated fat 7g, fibre 2g, sugar 40g, salt 0.16g

Greengages have the perfect combination of sweetness and acidity that you need for a fruit tart, plus a great dramatic colour. If you can't find greengages, use small plums instead.

Greengage and vanilla tart

375g pack dessert pastry
450g/1lb greengages, halved and stoned
3 tbsp caster sugar
2 medium eggs
1 tsp vanilla extract
142ml pot single cream
icing sugar, for dusting

Takes 1¼ hours • Serves 8

1 Preheat oven to 200°C/fan 180°C/gas 6. Roll out the pastry and use to line a shallow, loose-bottomed flan tin, about 24cm wide. Trim the edges and line with baking paper and baking beans. Sit it on a baking sheet, bake for 15 minutes, remove the paper and beans, then bake for 5 minutes more until pale golden and biscuity.
2 Meanwhile, put the greengages into a roasting tin, sprinkle with 1 tablespoon of the sugar, then roast until just softened. Drain off any juices, and cool.
3 Arrange the greengages in the pastry case, cut-side up and reduce the oven temperature to 160°C/fan 140°C/gas 3. Lightly whisk the eggs, then whisk in the vanilla extract, remaining sugar, and cream. Pour the egg mixture around the fruit, then bake for 30 minutes until set.
4 Cool the tart in the tin for 10 minutes, then remove to a plate and dust with icing sugar.

• Per serving 327 kcalories, protein 5g, carbohydrate 35g, fat 20g, saturated fat 8g, fibre 2g, sugar 18g, salt 0.3g

The perfect summer dessert for a crowd.

Raspberry tart with almond pastry

FOR THE PASTRY
200g/8oz plain flour
175g/6oz ground almonds
175g/6oz golden caster sugar
200g/8oz cold butter, diced
1 egg yolk

FOR THE FILLING
200ml pot crème fraîche
85g/3oz golden caster sugar
½ tsp vanilla essence
juice and zest of ½ lemon
about 700g/1lb 9oz raspberries

FOR THE GLAZE
5 tbsp raspberry jam

Takes 1 hour 10 minutes, plus cooling
Serves 10

1 Tip all the pastry ingredients, except the egg yolk, into a processor and pulse to the texture of breadcrumbs. Add the egg yolk, then pulse again to form a soft pastry. It will be too soft to roll, so press the pastry evenly into a loose-based 25cm tart tin until it comes up above the edges of the tin. Freeze for 30 minutes.
2 Preheat oven to 190°C/fan 170°C/gas 5. Line the pastry with baking paper and baking beans, place on a baking sheet and bake for 20 minutes. Remove the beans and paper, and bake for 10 minutes until biscuity. Cool, trim the edges, then remove from the tart tin.
3 Whisk the crème fraîche, sugar, vanilla essence, lemon juice and zest until thick. Spread inside the tart case, then top with raspberries. Warm the jam with 2 tablespoons of water until bubbling. Sieve, then paint it over the raspberries with a pastry brush.

• Per serving 659 kcalories, protein 8g, carbohydrate 63g, fat 43g, saturated fat 22g, fibre 4g, sugar 48g, salt 0.36g

Baking a cheesecake in a rectangle not only looks impressive but makes it much easier to serve too. The sticky cherries also make a great low-fat compote to serve with frozen yogurt or ice cream.

Cherry cheesecake slice

FOR THE BASE
200g pack shortbread biscuits, finely crushed
50g/2oz butter, melted

FOR THE CAKE
600g soft cheese
1 tsp vanilla extract
175g/6oz golden caster sugar
2 tbsp plain flour
2 eggs

FOR THE TOPPING
50g/2oz golden caster sugar
400g/14oz cherries, pitted

Takes 1 hour 20 minutes, plus cooling
Serves 8

1 Preheat oven to 160°C/fan 140°C/gas 3. Grease and line a loose-sided metal terrine tin (27x10cmx7cm), or a similar-sized loaf tin, with baking paper. Mix the shortbread crumbs and butter well, then press into the base of the tin.
2 Beat the cheese, vanilla extract and sugar until smooth, then beat in the flour and eggs until combined. Pour the mix over the base and smooth the top. Bake for 1 hour or until just set in the middle and tinged brown. Cool, then chill until completely cold.
3 For the topping, sprinkle the sugar into a frying pan and set over a high heat until caramelised. Add the cherries and stew for 3–4 minutes until they're sticky and juicy. Remove the cherries with a slotted spoon and set aside. Bubble down the juices to a sticky syrup. Cool.
4 To serve, release the cheesecake from the tin and leave at room temperature for 30 minutes. Top with the cherries and syrup before serving.

• Per serving 533 kcalories, protein 9g, carbohydrate 57g, fat 32g, saturated fat 19g, fibre 1g, sugar 42g, salt 1.09g

If you're ever stuck for what to do with gooseberries, think of a classic
lemon dessert and simply swap the lemon for these tangy berries.

Gooseberry meringue tart

375g pack shortcrust dessert pastry
50g/2oz butter
100g/4oz light muscovado sugar
500g/1lb 2oz gooseberries

FOR THE TOPPING
2 egg whites
100g/4oz caster sugar
1 tsp cornflour

Takes 1 hour 10 minutes • Serves 8

1 Preheat oven to 180°C/fan 160°C/gas 4.
Roll out the pastry on a lightly floured surface,
then use it to line a 23cm, loose-bottomed tart
tin. Line with baking paper and baking beans;
bake for 15 minutes. Remove the beans, then
bake for 10 minutes more until golden. Remove
from the oven, then reduce the temperature to
140°C/fan 120°C/gas 1.
2 Heat the butter and muscovado sugar in a
shallow pan. When the sugar has completely
dissolved, throw in the gooseberries and toss
them in the caramel. Cook for a few minutes
until they start to split and collapse. Cool, then
stir and tip into the pastry case.
3 For the topping, whisk the egg whites to soft
peaks. Whisk in the sugar a spoonful at a time,
then whisk in the cornflour. Blob the meringue
over the gooseberries and spread to cover.
Bake for about 40 minutes until the meringue is
cooked and lightly browned.

• Per serving 384 kcalories, protein 4g, carbohydrate
51g, fat 20g, saturated fat 8g, fibre 2.5g, sugar 32g,
salt 0.40g

This is ideal for using up a glut of summer berries after you've visited a pick-your-own farm, or when the supermarket has them on special offer.

Very berry ice

750g/1lb 10oz summer berries
140g/5oz caster sugar
juice of 1 lemon

Takes 15 minutes, plus cooling and freezing • Serves 6

1 Hull and chop the fruit, then tip into a bowl with the sugar and lemon juice. Pour over 300ml/½ pint of boiling water and leave everything to macerate until cool.

2 Blitz the mixture in a food processor until smooth. Push the purée through a sieve, then pour into a freezer-proof container and freeze until slushy around the edges, breaking up the crystals every 30 minutes or so. Once thick and semi-frozen, freeze for at least 4 hours or overnight.

• Per serving 126 kcalories, protein 1g, carbohydrate 32g, fat none, saturated fat none, fibre 2g, sugar 32g, salt 0.02g

Almonds and peaches are made for each other. These smart little tarts can be prepared and kept in the fridge for a few hours before baking.

Squashed peach and almond tarts

100g/4oz ground almonds
100g/4oz butter, softened, plus extra for greasing
1 egg
50g/2oz golden caster sugar
250g/9oz puff pastry
3 peaches, halved, stoned and finely sliced

Takes 50 minutes • Serves 4

1 Beat the almonds, butter, egg and half the sugar in a bowl until mixed. Roll out the pastry to the thickness of a 20p and, using a saucer about 13cm diameter, cut out four circles. Lift the circles onto a greased baking sheet and spread each thinly with 1 tablespoon of the almond mixture, leaving a border. Arrange the peach slices on top in a rosette and chill for at least 10 minutes before baking. Preheat oven to 220°C/fan 200°C/gas 7.
2 Bake the tarts on the top shelf for 10 minutes. Sprinkle liberally with the remaining sugar, cover with baking paper, and lay another baking sheet on the top. Flip the sheets so that the tarts are upside-down. Bake for 5–10 minutes more, until the pastry is crisp and the peaches are sticky and caramelized. (If you don't have two baking sheets, the tarts can be cooked peach-side up for the whole cooking time.)

• Per serving 672 kcalories, protein 12g, carbohydrate 44g, fat 51g, saturated fat 20g, fibre 3g, sugar 21g, salt 0.94g

Crisp choux pastry, fruit, cream and a wicked caramel sauce
make for a very special dinner-party dessert.

Fruity choux buns with caramel sauce

FOR THE PASTRY
85g/3oz butter
100g/4oz plain flour, sifted
pinch of salt
3 eggs, beaten

FOR THE CARAMEL SAUCE
50g/2oz butter
5 tbsp soft brown sugar
142ml carton double cream

FOR THE FILLING
142ml or 284ml carton double cream
(depending on how creamy you
like them)
1 tbsp icing sugar, sifted
3 tbsp dessert wine (sweet Muscat
works well)
2 ripe peaches, stoned and sliced
150g pack blueberries

Takes 40 minutes, plus cooling
Serves 6

1 Put the butter and 200ml of cold water into a medium pan and bring to a rolling boil. Take off the heat, immediately tip in the flour and salt. Beat with electric beaters to a smooth paste that leaves the sides of the pan. Cool on a plate.
2 Preheat oven to 200°C/fan 180°C/gas 6 and line a baking sheet with baking paper. Return the paste to the pan. Beat in the eggs little by little; stop when you have a shiny paste that drops easily from a spoon. Spoon on to the baking sheet in six large round blobs. Bake for 20–25 minutes, until dark golden. Make a hole in the base of each bun, then bake for 5 more minutes. Cool on a wire rack.
3 Heat the sauce ingredients together for 5 minutes, stirring, until silky.
4 To make the filling, softly whip together the cream, sugar and wine. Split the buns, spoon in the cream and fruit then serve with the sauce.

• Per serving (using 142ml cream) 589 kcalories, protein 7g, carbohydrate 34g, fat 48g, saturated fat 27g, fibre 2g, sugar 21g, salt 0.75g

Cheesecake is always a popular choice for parties – and this one's dead easy to make.

Baked vanilla and lemon cheesecake with raspberries

12 Petit Beurre or digestive biscuits, finely crushed
50g/2oz butter, melted
1 tbsp clear honey
500g tub ricotta cheese
3 eggs
175g/6oz caster sugar
grated zest of 1 lemon
2 tsp vanilla extract
200g pot crème fraîche
250–300g/9–10oz raspberries
icing sugar, for dusting

Takes about 1 hour, plus cooling
Serves 6 with leftovers

1 Mix the biscuits with the butter then press into a 20cm springform or loose-based cake tin. Preheat oven to 160°C/fan 140°C/gas 3.
2 Put the remaining ingredients, except the raspberries and icing sugar, into a food processor, and process until smooth. Pour into the tin and shake to level. Bake for 40 minutes, then turn off the oven and leave the cheesecake inside to cool for 1 hour. When completely cool, chill overnight. Don't worry if it has cracked on top, as this will be hidden by the raspberries.
3 Remove the cheesecake from the tin and put on a serving plate. Scatter over the raspberries and dust with icing sugar before serving.

• Per serving 639 kcalories, protein 15g, carbohydrate 61g, fat 39g, saturated fat 22g, fibre 2g, sugar 44g, salt 0.93g

If you're entertaining but short of time, this quick and simple summer dessert is just the thing.

Berry and lemon brandy baskets

150g punnet raspberries
6 tbsp fromage frais
2 tbsp lemon curd
4 ready-made brandy snap baskets
1 tbsp toasted flaked almonds

Takes 5 minutes • Serves 4

1 Reserve a few raspberries for decoration, then put the rest in a bowl and mash roughly with a fork. Fold in the fromage frais and lemon curd, and divide the mixture among the brandy snap baskets. Top with the remaining raspberries and the almonds, then serve straight away.

• Per basket 159 kcalories, protein 3g, carbohydrate 21g, fat 8g, saturated fat 4g, fibre 1g, sugar 15g, salt 0.16g

Scoop your ice cream into balls, sit them on a baking sheet and freeze until you need them – it makes serving sundaes to lots of people really stress- and melt-free.

Boozy strawberry mess

600g/1lb 5oz strawberries
a splash of vodka (optional)
6 meringue nests
6 scoops strawberry or raspberry
ice cream

Takes 10 minutes • Serves 6

1 Hull all the strawberries then slice half and set aside. Roughly chop the rest, then mash with a fork. Spoon the mashed strawberries into four sundae dishes and splash over a little of the vodka, if you like.
2 Crumble the meringue nests over the mashed berries and scatter over the halved fruit. Add scoops of ice cream and serve straight away.

• Per serving 224 kcalories, protein 2.6g, carbohydrate 33.1g, fat 8.1g, saturated fat 5.1g, fibre 1.2g, sugar 32.4g, salt 0.16g

This quintessentially British pudding, packed with juicy summer berries, is so much easier to make than it appears.

Stunning summer pudding

175g/6oz golden caster sugar
1.25kg/2lb 12oz mixed berries and currants, washed (we used
250g/9oz blackberries
100g/4oz blackcurrants
100g/4oz redcurrants
500g/1lb 2oz raspberries
300g/10oz strawberries, quartered)
7 slices from a day-old, square, medium-cut white sliced loaf, crusts removed
extra berries and double cream, to serve

Takes 30 minutes, plus chilling
Serves 8

1 Dissolve the sugar in 3 tablespoons of water. Boil for 1 minute, then tip in all the fruit except the strawberries. Cook for 3 minutes until soft, stirring occasionally. Drain the juice into a bowl.
2 Line a 1.4 litre basin with cling film, letting it overhang. Cut 4 pieces of bread in half, a little on an angle. Cut 2 slices into 4 triangles each and leave the final piece whole.
3 Dip the whole piece of bread into the fruit juice and use to line the base of the bowl. Dip the bread halves in the juice and line the basin's sides. Spoon in the mixed fruit and strawberries.
4 Dip the bread triangles into the juice and use to cover the fruit. Keep any leftover juice. Cover the top of the bowl with the overhanding cling film. Weigh down using a plate and a couple of cans. Chill overnight. To serve, open the cling film and turn the pudding out on to a plate. Serve with leftover juice and extra berries.

• Per serving 248 kcalories, protein 6g, carbohydrate 57g, fat 1g, saturated fat none, fibre 9g, added sugar 43g, salt 0.45g

You can make these with very little time and effort, and they go equally well with a big pot of tea or a glass of fizz. When blackberries start to appear, they can be used instead of raspberries.

Raspberry and orange shortcakes

300g/10oz raspberries
100g/4oz butter, cut into small pieces
300g/10oz self-raising flour
zest and juice of 1 orange
85g/3oz caster sugar
200ml/7fl oz buttermilk or a half-and-half mix of natural low-fat yogurt and milk
icing sugar, for dusting
284ml pot whipping cream

Takes 40 minutes, plus freezing
Serves 8

1 Freeze a third of the raspberries for 30 minutes. Line a baking sheet with baking paper. In a bowl, rub the butter and flour together with your fingertips until it looks like fine crumbs. Add the orange zest, sugar and frozen raspberries, then lightly mix.
2 Stir in the buttermilk or yogurt mix, then combine quickly to form a soft dough.
3 Preheat oven to 200°C/fan 180°C/gas 6. Turn out onto a lightly floured surface and knead briefly. Roll or press out to a 2cm thickness, then stamp out into 8cm rounds. Transfer to the baking sheet and bake for 18–20 minutes until lightly golden. Cool on a wire rack, then dust with icing sugar.
4 Whip the cream lightly. Serve shortcakes split in half and topped with whipped cream and the remaining raspberries.

• Per serving 352 kcalories, protein 6g, carbohydrate 45g, fat 18g, saturated fat 11g, fibre 2g, sugar 17g, salt 0.6g

If you can, choose in-season, beautifully fragrant apricots for this stunning dessert.

Rosé-poached apricots with apricot ice cream

75cl bottle of rosé wine
140g/5oz caster sugar
1 vanilla pod, split
1kg/2lb 4oz apricots, halved and stoned
300ml pot fresh vanilla custard
284ml pot whipping cream

Takes 40 minutes, plus freezing
Serves 6

1 Heat the wine, sugar and vanilla pod until the sugar has dissolved, then add the apricots and poach gently until just softened. Cook in batches if this is easier. (Watch them, as they collapse easily and, ideally, you want them to keep their shape.)

2 Scoop half the apricots out of the pan using a slotted spoon (choose the softer ones for this). Transfer the firmer apricots into a separate bowl. Boil the juices hard for 3–4 minutes to make a light syrup. Cool a little, then pour over the firmer apricots and leave to cool.

3 Purée the softer apricots in a processor, then add the custard and cream, and mix well. Pour into a clean bowl, cool, then chill. Freeze for 3 hours, breaking down the crystals with a fork every half hour until thick and smooth. Freeze until solid. Serve scoops of ice cream with the poached apricots.

• Per serving 375 kcalories, protein 4g, carbohydrate 40g, fat 21g, saturated fat 13g, fibre 3g, sugar 40g, salt 0.11g

You can never have enough of this kind of summer dessert recipe in your repertoire – and, as it can be made ahead, it's ideal for entertaining.

Summer berry mousse cake

FOR THE BISCUIT BASE
200g/8oz digestive biscuits, crushed
100g/4oz butter, melted

FOR THE MOUSSE CAKE
4 sheets leaf gelatine
142ml pot single cream
500g pot fromage frais
140g/5oz golden caster sugar
zest 1 small orange
4 tbsp orange juice
400g/14oz raspberries, some crushed
284ml pot double cream

FOR THE SAUCE
250g mixture of strawberries (chopped)
and raspberries
3 tbsp orange juice
2 tbsp golden caster sugar

TO DECORATE
mixture of strawberries (some halved),
raspberries and blueberries
icing sugar, for dusting

Takes 45 mins, plus chilling • Serves 8

1 Stir the biscuits and butter together, then tip into a loose-bottomed 24cm cake tin. Press down evenly then chill.
2 For the mousse, soak the gelatine in a bowl of cold water for 5 mins. Bring the single cream to the boil, take off the heat. Lift the gelatine from water, squeeze out any excess then stir into the hot cream to dissolve. Cool for 5 mins.
3 Whisk together the fromage frais, sugar, orange zest and juice. Stir in the cream mixture and the whole and crushed raspberries.
4 Softly whip the double cream then fold into the raspberry mixture. Pour into the tin then chill 4 hrs, or overnight, until set.
5 Blitz all the sauce ingredients in a food processor, then chill. Serve the cake topped with fruit, a dusting of icing sugar and a little sauce.

• Per serving 607 kcalories, protein 10g, carbohydrate 53g, fat 41 g, saturated fat 24g, fibre 3g, sugar 28g, salt 0.76g

Bring back memories of traditional seaside ice-cream parlours
with this light, fruity sundae.

Fruity summer sundaes

142ml pot double cream
2 tbsp icing sugar
12 strawberries, 4 left whole,
rest chopped
4 nectarines, chopped into small
chunks
4 scoops good-quality vanilla
ice cream
4 scoops good-quality berry sorbet

FOR THE MACADAMIA BRITTLE
sunflower oil, for greasing
50g/2oz macadamia nuts, toasted
50g/2oz caster sugar

FOR THE STRAWBERRY SAUCE
350g/12oz strawberries, hulled
1 tbsp icing sugar

Takes 25 minutes, plus cooling
Serves 4 (easily doubled)

1 Make the brittle first. Oil a baking sheet, spread over the nuts, and set aside. Gently heat the caster sugar in a small non-stick frying pan, stirring until dissolved. When the sugar becomes a deep caramel, pour over the nuts, then leave until completely cold. Snap the brittle into pieces, then pulse in a food processor to coarse crumbs. (The brittle can be made up to a week ahead and stored in an airtight container.)
2 For the sauce, whiz the strawberries in a food processor until smooth. Sieve into a bowl, then stir in the icing sugar. Set aside.
3 To assemble the sundaes, whip the cream with the icing sugar until it just holds its shape. Layer up the chopped fruit, brittle, ice cream, sorbet and sauce in four glasses, finishing with swirls of cream, more brittle and the whole strawberries.

• Per serving 609 kcalories, protein 7g, carbohydrate 71g, fat 35g, saturated fat 15g, fibre 4g, sugar 69g, salt none

Once made, this is a great stand-by that can be pulled out of the freezer at a moment's notice.

Frozen banana and peanut butter cheesecake

3 small bananas
50g/2oz butter, melted
10 digestive biscuits, crushed to crumbs
142ml pot double cream
140g/5oz icing sugar
400g tub soft cheese
½ tsp vanilla extract
237g jar crunchy peanut butter

Takes 30 minutes, plus freezing
Serves 8–10

1 Several hours ahead, put 2 bananas in the freezer until the skins go black, then remove and defrost – you'll be left with really soft bananas. Peel, then mash well.
2 Next, mix together the butter and biscuits, then press into a 23cm springform cake tin. Whip the cream until it just holds its shape. In a separate bowl, beat the sugar, soft cheese and vanilla extract together until completely combined. In another bowl, beat the peanut butter to loosen it.
3 Fold the cheese mixture into the peanut butter, then tip in the mashed banana and gently fold in the cream. Spread over the biscuit base and smooth the top. Freeze for 6 hours, or preferably overnight. To serve, transfer to the fridge for 20 minutes, then run a knife around the side and unclip the tin. Slice the remaining banana and use to decorate the cheesecake.

• Per serving (8) 624 kcalories, protein 12g, carbohydrate 43g, fat 46g, saturated fat 21g, fibre 3g, sugar 30g, salt 1.18g

This iced terrine will sit happily in the freezer for up to a month, ready to slice when you need it.

Crunchy raspberry ripple terrine

350g/12oz raspberries
3 eggs
100g/4oz golden caster sugar
284ml pot double cream
2 meringue nests, crushed into small pieces

Takes 25 minutes, plus freezing
Serves 8

1 Mash 150g of the raspberries, pass through a sieve into a bowl, discarding the seeds, and set aside. Line a 1-litre loaf tin with cling film. Using electric beaters, whisk the eggs and sugar continuously over a pan of barely simmering water, until doubled in volume and thick. Remove bowl from heat. Continue to whisk until completely cool; the whole process will take about 10 minutes.
2 Whisk the cream until just thick. Fold the egg mix into the cream until completely combined, then fold in the meringues. Pour the raspberry purée over the mix in a zigzag, then gently pour into the lined loaf tin. Freeze for at least 4 hours and serve in slices with the remaining whole raspberries.

• Per serving 284 kcalories, protein 4g, carbohydrate 19g, fat 22g, saturated fat 11g, fibre 1g, sugar 19g, salt 0.11g

The vanilla in this recipe means that the whole dish works really well when served with strawberries.

Mango and vanilla granita

1 vanilla pod, split (optional)
140g/5oz caster sugar
2 large ripe mangoes
300g/10oz strawberries, sliced,
to serve

Takes 15 minutes, plus freezing
Serves 6–8

1 Tip the vanilla pod, into a bowl with the sugar, if using. Pour 250ml of boiling water over the sugar. Stir until completely dissolved, then leave to cool.

2 Meanwhile, peel the mangoes and cut away all the flesh, then blitz in a food processor until you have a smooth purée. Stir the purée into the sugar syrup and fish out the vanilla pod. Pour into a freezerproof container and freeze until slushy around the edges, breaking up the crystals every 30 minutes or so.

3 Once thick and semi-frozen, freeze for at least 4 hours or overnight. Alternatively, churn in an ice-cream machine to make a sorbet. Serve with sliced strawberries.

• Per serving (6) 163 kcalories, protein 1g, carbohydrate 42g, fat none, saturated fat none, fibre 3g, sugar 41g, salt 0.02g

Choosing pink-fleshed plums will give you the most stunning colour
in this winning prepare-ahead dessert for friends.

Plum kulfis

3 cardamom pods
700g/1lb 9oz plums, halved and
stoned
100g/4oz caster sugar
400ml can condensed milk
150ml/¼ pint milk
2 tbsp chopped pistachio nuts,
to sprinkle

Takes 35 minutes, plus freezing
Serves 6

1 Split the cardamom pods and remove the seeds, then crush the seeds with a pestle and mortar or the end of a rolling pin in a cup. Put in a pan with the plums, sugar and 5 tablespoons of water, then bring to the boil. Reduce the heat, cover, then cook for 10 minutes until the plums are very soft. Tip into a food processor and blend until smooth. Pour into a jug and leave to cool.

2 Mix together the condensed milk, milk and 300ml of the plum purée. Pour into six moulds, ramekins, plastic beakers or small cups, then freeze for 4 hours or until firm.

3 To serve, dip each mould briefly into hot water, then invert them on to six small plates. Pour a little plum purée around each kulfi and sprinkle with chopped pistachios.

• Per serving 365 kcalories, protein 8g, carbohydrate 66g, fat 10g, saturated fat 5g, fibre 2g, sugar 66g, salt 0.27g

Basil and raspberry work brilliantly together in these special crème brûlées.

Iced raspberry and basil brûlées

225g punnet raspberries
50g/2oz golden caster sugar
142ml pot double cream
100ml/3½fl oz fresh custard
a handful of basil leaves, finely shredded
3 tbsp icing sugar

Takes 20 minutes, plus freezing
Serves 4

1 Divide the raspberries among four ramekins, then scatter over the sugar and press down lightly with the back of a spoon. Whip the cream until it holds its shape, then fold the custard and basil through the cream. Spoon the creamy mixture over the raspberries and smooth over the tops.

2 Leave the ramekins in the freezer for about 30 minutes to just set the cream – you don't want it set solid. (The creams can now be frozen for up to 2 weeks, but should be defrosted slightly in the fridge for a few hours before serving.)

3 To serve, dust each ramekin evenly with a layer of icing sugar, then use a blowtorch to caramelise the top. Leave the caramel to harden for 1 minute, then serve straight away.

• Per brûlées 329 kcalories, protein 2g, carbohydrate 36g, fat 20g, saturated fat 12g, fibre 1g, sugar 34g, salt 0.06g

You can use whatever fruit you wish in this ice cream,
depending on your preferred flavour of cheesecake.

Blackcurrant cheesecake ice cream

1 plump vanilla pod, split and seeds
scraped out
300ml/1½ pints full-fat milk
300ml/1½ pints double cream
100g/4oz golden caster sugar
4 egg yolks
150g tub cream cheese, beaten
100g/4oz blackcurrant conserve
5–6 shortbread biscuits, crumbled
into chunks

Takes 35 minutes, plus cooling,
churning and freezing • Serves 6

1 In a pan, mix the vanilla seeds and pod
with the milk and cream. Bring to the boil, then
leave off the heat for 30 minutes or until cold.
2 In a large bowl, whisk together the sugar
and egg yolks for a few minutes until pale
and fluffy. Put the vanilla cream back on the
heat until just about to boil, then sieve on to
the yolks, whisking until completely mixed.
3 Pour the custard back into the pan and
cook on the lowest heat, stirring continuously,
paying attention to the corners, for about
10 minutes until you can draw a line through
the mix on the back of the spoon. Tip into
a container, stir in the cheese, then cool.
4 Freeze until slushy around the edges,
breaking up the edges every so often until
semi-frozen. Spoon in dollops of conserve
and chunks of biscuit, and fold through.
Freeze until solid.

• Per serving 587 kcalories, protein 8g, carbohydrate
44g, fat 44g, saturated fat 24g, fibre none, sugar 36g,
salt 0.48g

The beauty of this slush, apart from its special berry flavour,
is that you don't have to wait too long until you can dig in!

Raspberry and red wine slush with peach salad

225g punnet raspberries
400ml/14fl oz light red wine (such as
Beaujolais)
140g/5oz caster sugar
2 ripe peaches, halved, stoned and
cut into wedges
a handful of mint leaves

Takes 20 minutes, plus freezing
Serves 4

1 Tip the raspberries, wine and sugar into a blender and blitz until smooth (this can also be done in a large jug with a hand blender). Push the liquid through a sieve to get rid of some of the seeds, then churn in an ice-cream machine until the texture of soft sorbet.
2 If you don't have an ice-cream machine, transfer the liquid to a freezer-proof container and freeze until it starts to become icy, then mash the ice crystals with a fork until slushy. Repeat 3–4 times until you have the texture of sorbet. Keep in the freezer until you are ready to use.
3 To serve, toss the peaches with the mint and serve alongside bowls of the scooped slush.

• Per serving 240 kcalories, protein 2g, carbohydrate 44g, fat none, saturated fat none, fibre 2g, sugar 43g, salt 0.03g

Wow family and friends with this spectacular pudding – a true treat for summer.

Mango, lime and blackberry bombe

2 × 200g punnets blackberries
250g/9oz icing sugar
2 × 425g cans mango in syrup, juice reserved
zest and juice of 4 limes
142ml pot and 285ml pot double cream
2 crushed brandy snaps, to serve

Takes 30 minutes, plus freezing
Serves 10

1 Put the blackberries in pan with 4 tablespoons of the sugar, add a splash of water and cook until softened. Push through a sieve, cool, then freeze in a plastic container until slushy, stirring every now and then.
2 Whiz the mango with 75ml of its syrup and 2 tablespoons of the icing sugar until smooth, then freeze in a container until slushy, as above.
3 Mix the rest of the sugar with the lime zest and juice. Beat the cream with 3 tablespoons of the remaining mango syrup until it forms soft peaks, then beat in the lime mixture. Freeze in a container until semi-frozen.
4 Line a medium basin with cling film then beat all three icy mixtures and spoon alternately into the bowl to make rippled layers. Freeze until solid.
5 Leave for 30 minutes in the fridge before eating then serve scattered with the crushed biscuits.

• Per serving 400 kcalories, protein 1g, carbohydrate 48g, fat 23g, saturated fat 13g, fibre 2g, sugar 47g, salt 0.06g

Everyone loves a lolly on a hot day. These tropical coolers are really easy and quick to make, and you can pick up lolly moulds and sticks in most supermarkets.

Guava and passion fruit lollies

300ml/10fl oz passion fruit juice
300ml/10fl oz guava juice

Takes 5 minutes, plus freezing
Makes 8

1 Pour the passion fruit juice into eight lolly moulds, and freeze until almost solid.
2 Push a lolly stick into each mould, then top up with the guava juice. Freeze until solid.

• Per lolly 32 kcalories, protein 0.5g, carbohydrate 8.0g, fat none, saturated fat none, fibre 2g, sugar 8.0g, salt 0.02g

Sweetshop flavours come together in these lip-smacking lollies.

Raspberry–coconut ices

140g/5oz raspberries
4 tbsp icing sugar
450g pot Greek-style coconut yogurt

Takes 15 minutes, plus freezing
Makes 8

1 Put the raspberries into a food processor with the sugar, then whiz to a purée. Push through a sieve into a bowl to remove the seeds. Spoon half of the yogurt into a bowl, and ripple in 2 tablespoons of the raspberry purée.
2 Spoon the pink yogurt mix into eight lolly moulds, divide the rest of the purée among the moulds, then top up each with the rest of the yogurt. Push in lolly sticks and freeze until solid.

• Per ice 123 kcalories, protein 2.3g, carbohydrate 14.7g, fat 6.4g, saturated fat 4.7g, fibre 0.6g, sugar 14.7g, salt 0.06g

These granitas are beautifully scented and cooling. If you don't like rose water, use elderflower cordial instead.

Fruity granitas

MELON AND ROSE GRANITA
1 ripe melon, such as Ogen, halved and seeded
140g/5oz golden caster sugar
few drops of rosewater (elderflower cordial can be used instead)
fresh rose petals, to decorate (optional)

LEMONADE GRANITA
3 unwaxed lemons
140g/5oz golden caster sugar
lemon zest strips, to decorate

Takes 20 minutes plus freezing
Serves 4

1 For the melon and rose granita, purée the melon flesh, sugar and rosewater in a food processor. Add 600ml/1 pint water and blend until smooth. Rub the mixture through a sieve into a plastic container. Freeze for 3 hours, until partially frozen. Beat with a fork, then freeze again. Beat occasionally until icy and slushy. Alternatively, use an ice-cream machine. Serve decorated with rose petals.
2 For the lemonade granita, blend the lemons, sugar and 600ml/1 pint water in a food processor. Sieve into a bowl, pressing out the juice. Freeze in a shallow container. When frozen, break into chunks and blend until smooth. Freeze for 2 hours until icy. Decorate with lemon zest to serve.

• Melon and Rose per portion 170 kcalories, protein 1.1g, carbohydrates 43.6g, fat 0.3g, saturated fat 0g, fibre 1.7g, sugar 43.6g, salt 0.04g • Lemonade per portion 151 kcalories, protein 0.7g, carbohydrate 38.9g, fat 0.2g, saturated fat 0g, fibre 0g, added sugar 38.9g, salt 0.01g

Kulfi is usually made with milk boiled for several hours. This sneaky version made with condensed milk does all the hard work for you.

Rose water and pistachio kulfi with griddled mangoes

450g squeezy tube condensed milk
2 tbsp rose water
50g/2oz very finely chopped
pistachio nuts, plus roughly
chopped extras to serve
284ml pot double cream
3 small ripe mangoes
limes, for squeezing (optional)

Takes 25 minutes, plus freezing
Serves 6

1 Squeeze the condensed milk into a bowl and beat in the rose water and finely chopped pistachios. Lightly whip the cream until it holds its shape, then fold into the pistachio mixture.
2 Pour into six small ramekins or dariole moulds. Cover with cling film, then freeze.
3 Slice each mango on either side of the stone to make six halves, but don't peel. Score a criss-cross into the flesh, but don't slice through the skin. Cook on the barbecue or a hot griddle, flesh-side down, until starting to caramelize. Leave as it is or turn inside out to make the segments stand proud. Serve with the kulfi, scattered with the extra pistachios (and a squeeze of lime, if you like).

• Per serving 601 kcalories, protein 10g, carbohydrate 60g, fat 38g, saturated fat 20g, fibre 3g, sugar 59g, salt 0.30g

This couldn't be simpler – no machine, no churning. Wild strawberries have an intense flavour, but ordinary strawberries will work well too, providing they're in season and properly ripe.

Wild strawberry ice cream

200g/8oz wild strawberries
140g/5oz golden caster sugar
200ml/7fl oz dessert wine
500ml pot crème fraîche

Takes 15 minutes, plus freezing
Serves 6

1 Scatter two-thirds of the strawberries into a shallow dish. Sprinkle with 50g of the sugar and all of the wine, then leave the strawberries to macerate while you whisk the crème fraîche.

2 Tip the rest of sugar and the crème fraîche into a bowl, and whisk until thick. Use a spatula to fold the strawberries and wine into the crème fraîche. Spoon into a rigid container and freeze for at least 4 hours until scoopable. Serve in chilled bowls, scattered with the remaining strawberries.

• Per serving 448 kcalories, protein 2g, carbohydrate 31g, fat 33g, saturated fat 22g, fibre none, sugar 31g, salt 0.07g

Turn a few humble cans of lychees into a wonderfully fragrant dessert. If you don't want to add the egg white the flavour will be the same, but the texture will be more grainy.

Refreshing lychee and lime sorbet

3 × 400g cans lychees in syrup
50g/2oz caster sugar
zest of 2 limes, juice of 1
1 egg white

Takes 25 minutes, plus freezing
Serves 6

1 Drain the syrup from two of the cans of lychees into a small pan. Add the sugar and dissolve over a gentle heat. Bring to the boil for 1 minute.
2 Blitz the drained lychees in a food processor until very finely chopped. Pour in the lime juice and syrup with the blade still whirring – don't worry if the mix isn't perfectly smooth at this point. Tip into a 1-litre freezer-proof container and freeze for at least 6 hours until solid.
3 Break up the frozen mix, then return to the bowl of the processor. Tip in the egg white and whiz until thick, pale and smooth. Add the zest from one of the limes. Return to the container and freeze again, ideally overnight. Serve in scoops with the remaining lychees and the rest of the lime zest scattered over.

• Per serving 137 kcalories, protein 1g, carbohydrate 35g, fat none, saturated fat none, fibre 1g, sugar 35g, salt 0.04g

This is a great no-cook pudding. Make sure you transfer it to the fridge before serving for the best flavour and texture.

Raspberry meringue ice-cream cake

175g/6oz icing sugar
500g tub fresh custard
500ml pot crème fraîche
2 tsp vanilla extract
400g/14oz raspberries, half crushed
100g/4oz meringues or meringue nests, broken into small chunks
300g jar raspberry coulis or sauce

Takes 20 minutes, plus freezing
Serves 8

1 Reserve 1 tablespoon of the sugar and mix the rest of the sugar with the custard, crème fraîche and vanilla extract. Freeze until semi-frozen. Whisk to break down the ice crystals, return to the freezer for 1 hour more, then repeat.
2 Meanwhile, oil and line a large loaf tin with cling film. Mix the crushed raspberries with the reserved sugar.
3 Spoon one-third of the custard mix into the tin. Sprinkle with half the meringues and half the crushed raspberries. Spoon over 3 tablespoons of the coulis. Cover with another third of the custard, remaining meringues, raspberries and 3 tablespoons coulis. Spoon over the remaining custard then freeze for at least 4 hours or overnight.
4 To serve, transfer to the fridge for 30–45 minutes to soften. When ready to eat, turn out onto a plate, scatter with raspberries, slice and serve with a little coulis.

• Per serving 468 kcalories, protein 4g, carbohydrate 52g, fat 29g, saturated fat 19g, fibre 1g, sugar 48g, salt 0.16g

If you're not into traditional Christmas pud, then try this brandy-soaked Christmas bombe instead, topped with a contrasting warm brandy–cranberry butter sauce.

Brandied Christmas bombe

100g/4oz raisins
100g/4oz sultanas
85g pack dried cranberries
6 tbsp brandy
2 tbsp dark muscovado sugar
284ml pot double cream
1 tbsp icing sugar
600ml pot good-quality fresh vanilla custard
100g/4oz frozen cranberries (keep them frozen)

FOR THE BRANDY–CRANBERRY BUTTER SAUCE
85g/3oz light muscovado sugar
175g/6oz butter
2 tbsp brandy
100g/4oz frozen cranberries

Takes 25 minutes, plus overnight soaking and freezing • Serves 8

1 Mix the dried fruit with 2 tablespoons of brandy and the sugar in a bowl, then cover with cling film. Microwave on High for 2 minutes until the sugar has melted and the fruit plumped up. Stir, then soak overnight.
2 Put the cream, remaining brandy and icing sugar into a bowl and softly whip. Fold into the custard. Freeze for 4 hours in a freezer-proof bowl, stirring in the edges every hour. Line a 1.2-litre pudding basin with cling film.
3 Quickly fold the soaked fruit, any liquid and the frozen cranberries through the ice cream, then tip into the lined pudding basin. Freeze for at least 6 hours.
4 For the sauce, heat the sugar and butter until the sugar dissolves. Add the brandy and cranberries. Simmer until the cranberries colour the sauce. Take the bombe out of the freezer. Leave for 10 minutes before turning out. Pour over the warm sauce to serve.

• Per serving 411 kcalories, protein 3g, carbohydrate 43g, fat 24g, saturated fat 14g, fibre 1g, sugar 40g, salt 0.14g

This light and refreshing ice makes a very elegant dessert
when scattered with a few mint leaves.

Vanilla yogurt ice with honeyed grapefruit

200g/8oz golden caster sugar
1 vanilla pod, seeds scraped out
2 × 500g pots natural yogurt

FOR THE HONEYED GRAPEFRUIT
3 pink grapefruit
4 tbsp clear honey
mint leaves, to serve

Takes 25 minutes, plus freezing
Serves 6

1 Put the caster sugar in a bowl, then rub in the vanilla seeds with your fingers so they are evenly mixed. Stir in the yogurt until the sugar has dissolved. Pour the yogurt into a freezer-proof container and freeze for 4–6 hours, stirring thoroughly every hour or so.

2 Line a 1kg-loaf tin with cling film. Spoon the soft frozen yogurt into the tin, cover with another piece of cling film, then freeze for at least 4 hours more, until firm.

3 Segment the grapefruit, catching the juices in a bowl (you should get about 200ml), discarding the pith. Put the juice into a small pan with the honey, simmer for 10–15 minutes until syrupy, stir in the segments, then leave to cool.

4 Take the yogurt ice from the freezer about 10 minutes before serving. Cut into slices and serve topped with grapefruit, some of the honeyed sauce and a scattering of mint leaves.

• Per serving 301 kcalories, protein 8g, carbohydrate 60g, fat 5 g, saturated fat 3g, fibre none, sugar 60g, salt 0.29g

You can use just one variety of plum for this simple dessert or choose a mixture of colours and flavours. The roasted plums can be kept in the fridge for up to 3 days and are delicious for breakfast, too.

Star anise-roasted plums

700g/1lb 9oz plums or a mix of plums, greengages and mirabelles
juice of 2 large oranges
3 star anise
3–4 tbsp maple syrup
mascarpone or Greek yogurt, to serve

Takes 45 minutes • Serves 4

1 Preheat oven to 180°C/fan 160°C/gas 4. Arrange the plums in a single layer in a large gratin dish. Pour over the orange juice, tuck star anise among the plums, drizzle over the syrup, then gently stir. Bake for 30–35 minutes until the fruit is soft but not collapsed.
2 Serve warm or cold with a dollop of mascarpone or yogurt on the side.

• Per serving (without mascarpone or yogurt)
101 kcalories, protein 1g, carbohydrate 25g, fat none, saturated fat none, fibre 3g, sugar 24g, salt 0.01g

Clementines are just the right size to top these little puddings.
If you like, you can make one big pudding – just increase
the cooking time to 50 minutes.

Sticky clementine and ginger puddings

3 clementines
140g/5oz butter, softened, plus extra
for greasing
6 tbsp golden syrup
175g/6oz golden caster sugar
3 eggs, beaten
140g/5oz self-raising flour
85g/3oz ground almonds
a pinch of ground ginger
2 balls stem ginger, finely chopped
cream or custard, to serve

Takes 50 minutes • Serves 6

1 Preheat oven to 200°C/fan 180°C/gas 6.
Juice one of the clementines and set aside. Peel
the other two, reserving the peel, then slice into
six thick rounds. Using a teaspoon, scrape away
the pith from the reserved peel, then finely chop
it and reserve.
2 Grease six individual pudding basins, drizzle
1 tablespoon of the golden syrup into each, add
a slice of clementine, then set aside.
3 In a bowl, beat the butter and sugar together
until pale, then beat in the eggs. Fold in the flour,
almonds, ground ginger and chopped peel,
then fold through the clementine juice and the
chopped ginger. Divide among the basins, then
cover each tightly with a greased hat of foil.
4 Put the basins in a roasting tin, half-fill the tin
with boiling water, then bake in the oven for
30 minutes until puffed up. Turn out on to plates
and serve with cream or custard.

• Per serving 563 kcalories, protein 9g, carbohydrate
66g, fat 31g, saturated fat 14g, fibre 2g, sugar 49g,
salt 0.80g

All the characteristics of a crumble, but a whole lot quicker.
This would make an ideal pud for a chilly autumn night.

Crunchy spiced plums

2 tbsp sugar
2 star anise
8 large or 12 small plums, halved
and stoned
a knob of butter
4 Hobnob biscuits
custard or vanilla ice cream, to serve

Takes 20 minutes • Serves 4

1 Preheat oven to 200°C/fan 180°C/gas 6.
Mix the sugar with 2 tablespoons of water in
a baking dish, add the star anise, then pop
in the plums, cut-side down. They should fit
quite snugly. Dot with the butter. Roast for
about 5 minutes until the plums are starting
to soften on the bottom, then turn them over.
Roast for another 5 minutes or until tender
(the time this takes depends on how ripe
the fruit is).
2 Roughly crush the Hobnobs, then spoon
a little on top of each plum half. Return to the
oven for a few minutes more until the biscuit
topping takes on a dark gold colour. Serve
the plums and their scented, syrupy juices
with custard or ice cream.

• Per serving 169 kcalories, protein 2g, carbohydrate
31g, fat 5g, saturated fat 2g, fibre 3g, sugar 25g,
salt 0.18g

Yorkshire pudding batter makes a wonderful dessert when paired with apples and blackberries. A perfect end to a Sunday lunch.

Blackberry and apple Yorkshire puddings

25g/1oz butter
140g/5oz golden caster sugar
4 eating apples (Cox's are good),
peeled, cored and cut into
bite-sized chunks
1 egg white
2 eggs
140g/5oz plain flour
200ml/7fl oz full-fat milk
150g punnet blackberries
2 tbsp sunflower oil
custard or vanilla ice cream, to serve

Takes 40 minutes • Serves 6

1 Preheat oven to 240°C/fan 220°C/gas 9. Heat the butter and 100g of the sugar in a frying pan, throw in the apples and cook over a high heat for 3–4 minutes until slightly caramelized and just starting to soften. Set aside.

2 In a clean bowl, whisk the egg white until frothy, then whisk in the rest of the sugar, the whole eggs, the flour and the milk. Stir the apples and the blackberries into the batter.

3 Add a splash of oil to each well of a six-hole, non-stick Yorkshire pudding tin then heat in the oven for 10 minutes. Once hot, quickly and carefully spoon a large ladleful of batter into each hole, making sure all the fruit is used. Bake for 15 minutes, without opening the door, until puffed up and golden. Serve straight away with custard or vanilla ice cream.

• Per serving 332 kcalories, protein 7g, carbohydrate 55g, fat 11g, saturated fat 4g, fibre 3g, sugar 37g, salt 0.21g

The strawberry jam and rhubarb in this easy, hot pud complement each other brilliantly.

Sticky rhubarb and strawberry sponge pudding

FOR THE TOPPING
140g/5oz rhubarb, cut into chunky lengths
2 tsp golden caster sugar
8 tbsp strawberry conserve

FOR THE SPONGE
140g/5oz softened butter, plus extra for greasing
140g/5oz self-raising flour
140g/5oz golden caster sugar
1 tsp baking powder
2 eggs
3 tbsp milk
¼ tsp vanilla essence
custard, to serve

Takes 1 hour 40 minutes • Serves 6

1 Lightly butter a 1.2-litre pudding basin. Mix the rhubarb, sugar and 2 teaspoons water in a small pan, and cook for 5 minutes until the sugar has dissolved and the rhubarb has softened slightly. Drain, reserving the juices, then mix the rhubarb with 4 tablespoons of the strawberry conserve. Spoon into the pudding basin. Preheat oven to 200°C/fan 180°C/gas 6.
2 Beat all the sponge ingredients together until light and creamy. Spoon on top of the rhubarb, then smooth the top.
3 Butter a sheet of foil, pleat it in the middle, then use to cover the pudding. Sit the basin in a roasting tin, half-fill the tin with just-boiled water, then bake for 50 minutes. It's ready when a skewer inserted in the centre comes out clean.
4 To serve, heat the reserved rhubarb juices with the remaining strawberry conserve. Turn out the pudding, drizzle the hot sauce over the top and enjoy with custard.

• Per serving 445 kcalories, protein 5g, carbohydrate 59g, fat 23g, saturated fat 13g, fibre 1g, sugar 41g, salt 0.93g

A warming dessert ready in just 10 minutes – now that's
what you need on a cold winter's weeknight.

Warm berry compote

a knob of butter
2 tbsp caster sugar
1 tsp vanilla extract
450g bag frozen summer berries,
defrosted
vanilla ice cream, to serve

Takes 10 minutes • Serves 4

1 Melt the butter over a low heat. Stir in the
sugar and vanilla extract, and heat gently until
the sugar melts.
2 Turn up the heat, then toss in the fruit.
Give the pan a good shake, then cook for
2–3 minutes until the fruit has warmed
through. Serve in bowls, spooned over vanilla
ice cream.

• Per serving 233 kcalories, protein 4g, carbohydrate
32g, fat 11g, saturated fat 7g, fibre 2g, sugar 31g,
salt 0.18g

Traditional Christmas pudding is easy to make – just stir it all together and steam. This can be made up to 1 month in advance and kept in the basin. It's gluten-free too!

Classic Christmas pudding

125g/4½oz raisins
125g/4½oz sultanas
200g/8oz currants
50g/2oz candied peel
50g/2oz glacé cherries, quartered
50g/2oz blanched almonds, chopped
4 tbsp brandy
125ml/4½fl oz gluten-free dark beer
125g/4½oz unsalted butter, softened, plus extra for greasing
225g/8½oz dark muscovado sugar
2 eggs, beaten
1 tsp ground mixed spice
½ tsp ground cinnamon
a grating of fresh nutmeg
100g/4oz ground almonds
1 tsp gluten-free baking powder
zest of 1 orange and 1 lemon
1 Bramley apple, peeled and grated

Takes about 5 hours, including 4½ hours steaming • Serves 8

1 Tip the dried fruit, almonds, brandy and beer into a medium-sized pan, and heat for 2 minutes until the fruit has started to absorb the liquid. Cool.
2 In a large bowl, beat together the butter, sugar, eggs, spices and almonds. Fold in the remaining ingredients and the soaked fruit.
3 Butter a 1.2-litre pudding basin and place a buttered disc of baking parchment in the bottom. Spoon the mix into the basin and cover with a pleated square of greaseproof paper and foil. Tie with string, then cut off any excess paper and foil. Place in a deep pan and pour enough boiling water to come two-thirds of the way up the sides of the bowl. Simmer, covered, for 4½ hours, topping up the water as necessary.
4 Let the pudding rest for 20 minutes before turning out. If made ahead, reheat in the microwave for 10 minutes on Medium or re-steam for 1 hour.

• Per serving 581 kcalories, protein 8g, carbohydrate 81g, fat 25g, saturated fat 10g, fibre 3g, sugar 78g, salt 0.37g

Ground rice gives the perfect, old-fashioned texture to this traditional steamed pud. If you can't get hold of ground rice, replace it with self-raising flour.

Cranberry-crowned pud

FOR THE TOPPING
140g/5oz fresh or frozen cranberries
200g jar redcurrant jelly
50g/2oz caster sugar

FOR THE SPONGE
200g/8oz butter, plus extra for greasing
175g/6oz self-raising flour
50g/2oz ground rice
1 tsp baking powder
200g/8oz golden caster sugar
4 eggs
seeds from 1 vanilla pod
custard, to serve

Takes about 2 hours, including 1½ hours steaming • Serves 8

1 Put 100g of the cranberries in a pan with the redcurrant jelly and sugar. Simmer for 5 minutes, then leave to cool. Meanwhile, put a pan of water on to simmer and butter a 1.4-litre pudding basin. Butter a large sheet of baking paper, sit on a same-size sheet of foil and fold a pleat in the middle. Beat all the sponge ingredients together, then stir in the remaining cranberries. Spoon a third of the cranberry and redcurrant mix into the bowl, then spoon the sponge mix on top.
2 Cover with the paper and foil, tie with string and steam, lid on, for 1½ hours. To serve, reheat the remaining cranberry mix and pour over the top of the turned-out pudding. (Can be made up to 2 days ahead and re-steamed for 30 minutes or microwaved for 5 minutes on High.) Serve with custard.

• Per serving 650 kcalories, protein 9g, carbohydrate 88g, fat 32g, saturated fat 19g, fibre 1g, sugar 64g, salt 1.01g

This classic pud seemed terribly glamorous when it was first popular in the 60s. It is now a little retro, but it still makes a great, economical family treat.

Pineapple upside-down cake

FOR THE TOPPING
50g/2oz softened butter
50g/2oz light muscovado sugar
7 pineapple rings in syrup, drained
and syrup reserved
about 7 glacé cherries

FOR THE CAKE
100g/4oz softened butter
100g/4oz golden caster sugar
100g/4oz self-raising flour
1 tsp baking powder
1 tsp vanilla extract
2 eggs
ice cream, to serve

Takes 55 minutes • Serves 6

1 Preheat oven to 180°C/160°C fan/gas 4. For the topping, beat the butter and sugar until creamy. Spread over the base and a quarter of the way up the sides of a 20cm round cake tin. Arrange the pineapple rings on top, then place cherries in the centres of the rings.
2 Put the cake ingredients in a bowl along with 2 tablespoons of the reserved pineapple syrup and, using an electric whisk, beat to a soft consistency.
3 Spoon into the tin on top of the pineapple and smooth it out so it's level. Bake for 35 minutes. Leave to stand for 5 minutes, then turn out on to a plate, with the pineapple slices on top. Serve warm with a scoop of ice cream.

• Per serving 407 kcalories, protein 5g, carbohydrate 49g, fat 23g, saturated fat 14g, fibre 1g, sugar 36g, salt 0.87g

Break into the pastry and you'll find a pool of
toffee fig sauce – perfect with a scoop of vanilla ice cream.

Toffee fig pies

500g block shortcrust pastry
6 fresh figs
6 hard toffees (we used Werther's
Original)
1 egg, beaten with a little milk
golden caster sugar, for scattering
vanilla ice cream, to serve

Takes 1 hour • Serves 6

1 Preheat oven to 200°C/fan 180°C/gas 6.
Roll out the pastry thinly on a floured surface.
Cut out six circles using a small saucer
(about 11–12cm diameter) and six circles
about half the size.
2 Cut the tops off the figs, squash them
down gently with your hands and push a
toffee into the centre of each one. Put a fig
in the middle of each large circle of pastry
and brush the egg around the pastry edge.
Brush the top of the fig with a little egg and
cover with the smaller circle of pastry. Pull
the edges of the larger circle up and pinch to
seal. Put on a greased baking sheet.
3 Brush the pies with more egg and scatter
over the sugar. Bake for 30–40 minutes until
golden and sticky. Cool for 10 minutes before
serving with ice cream.

• Per serving 458 kcalories, protein 7g, carbohydrate
52g, fat 26g, saturated fat 11g, fibre 2g, sugar 12g,
salt 0.96g

Dunk a spoon in when this pudding is cooked and the bottom will be covered with ever-so-slightly-tart apple slices and a rich toffee sauce.

Toffee apple pudding

85g/3oz butter, melted, plus extra
for greasing
140g/5oz self-raising flour
100g/4oz golden caster sugar
1 tbsp baking powder
200ml/7fl oz milk
1 egg, beaten
1 tsp vanilla extract
2 Bramley apples,
peeled, cored and sliced
pouring cream, warm custard
or vanilla ice cream, to serve

FOR THE SAUCE
140g/5oz soft dark brown sugar
50g/2oz pecan nuts roughly chopped

Takes 1 hour • Serves 6 (or 4 adults
and 4 kids)

1 Preheat oven to 180°C/fan 160°C/gas 4. Grease a large baking dish with butter. Tip the flour, sugar and baking powder, along with a pinch of salt, into a large bowl. Mix together the milk, butter, egg and vanilla extract, and stir into the dry ingredients to make a smooth batter. Arrange the apples in the dish, spoon over the batter and smooth with a knife until the apples are covered.

2 For the sauce, pour 250ml boiling water over the sugar and stir together until smooth. Pour the liquid over the pudding mixture, then scatter over the pecans. Bake for about 40 minutes until the pudding has risen and is golden. Use a big spoon to serve the pudding, making sure you get some of the gooey caramel sauce covering the bottom of the dish. Serve with pouring cream, warm custard or vanilla ice cream.

• Per serving (6) 452 kcalories, protein 6g, carbohydrate 68g, fat 20g, saturated fat 9g, fibre 2g, sugar 49g, salt 1.26g

This oaty topping will always have just the right amount of crumble and crunch – try it with apple, gooseberry or rhubarb too.

Maple plum crumble

8 ripe plums, halved and stoned
4 tbsp maple syrup
50g/2oz butter, cut into pieces
50g/2oz plain flour
50g/2oz rolled oats
25g/1oz golden caster sugar
½ tsp ground cinnamon
25g/1oz flaked almonds
custard, to serve

Takes 30 minutes • Serves 4

1 Preheat oven to 200°C/fan 180°C/gas 6. Arrange the plum halves, skin-side down, in the base of a large ovenproof dish. Drizzle over half the maple syrup and roast for 10 minutes.
2 Meanwhile, put the butter, flour, oats, sugar and cinnamon in a bowl, and rub the butter into the mixture until you have rough crumbs. Stir in the almonds, then sprinkle over the plums. Drizzle the top with the remaining maple syrup and bake for 15 minutes until the top is golden. Serve with custard.

• Per serving 325 kcalories, protein 5g, carbohydrate 45g, fat 15g, saturated fat 7g, fibre 4g, sugar 26g, salt 0.21g

Make more of rice pudding with seasonal fruit.

Apple and blackberry rice

425g can rice pudding
185g jar good-quality apple sauce
150g punnet blackberries (or use
frozen and defrost)
2 tbsp soft brown sugar

Takes 10 minutes • Serves 4

1 Heat the rice pudding then layer into four small dessert bowls or glasses, with the rice pudding, apple sauce and blackberries, finishing with a few blackberries on top.
2 Scatter with the brown sugar and leave for a few minutes until the sugar melts.

• Per serving 175 kcalories, protein 4g, carbohydrate 39g, fat 2g, saturated fat 1g, fibre 2g, sugar 31g, salt 0.14g

Add a bit of oomph to a can of pineapple for a fun and tasty dessert.

Hot passion piña coladas

4 thick slices pineapple (fresh
or from a can)
2 tbsp icing sugar
1 tbsp butter
2 tbsp rum or Malibu
4 scoops coconut ice cream
2 ripe passion fruit, halved

Takes 10 minutes • Serves 4

1 Dry the pineapple on kitchen paper, then dust on all sides with the icing sugar. Heat the butter in a non-stick frying pan, then add the pineapple slices and cook on both sides until golden and caramelized.

2 Add the rum or Malibu, then lift the pineapple on to plates and spoon over the juices. Top first with a scoop of ice cream while hot, then with the pulp from the passion fruit, scooped out with a teaspoon.

• Per serving 224 kcalories, protein 2.6g, carbohydrate 33.1g, fat 8.1g, saturated fat 5.1g, fibre 1.2g, sugar 32.4g, salt 0.16g

Serve this irresistible treacle tart for dessert while just warm –
perhaps with a drop of cool cream.

Gingery treacle tart with poached pears

500g pack sweet shortcrust pastry
a little flour, for dusting
300g/10oz granulated sugar
5 firm pears, peeled
zest of 3 lemons, juice of 1
600g/1lb 5oz golden syrup
1 ball stem ginger, finely chopped,
plus 1 tbsp syrup from the jar
2 eggs
140g/5oz breadcrumbs

Takes about 2 hours • Serves 8–10

1 Roll out the pastry with a little flour and line a loose-bottomed 23cm round tin. Leave excess pastry overhanging, then chill for 30 minutes.
2 In a large pan, melt the sugar in 800ml water. Simmer, then drop in the pears and the zest of one of the lemons. Cover, then poach for 12–15 minutes until almost tender. Lift out and set aside.
3 Preheat oven to 200°C/fan 180°C/gas 6. Line the tart with baking paper, fill with baking beans and bake for 15–20 minutes. Remove the paper and beans, and bake for 5 minutes more.
4 Warm the golden syrup with the remaining zest, the lemon juice and the ginger and its syrup. Stir in the eggs and crumbs.
5 Reduce oven temperature to 180°C/fan 160°C/gas 4. Slice the bottom off each pear and sit them upright in the tin. Spoon in the filling and bake for 50 minutes–1 hour until golden and set. Cool, trim the pastry edges, then serve.

• Per serving (8) 806 kcalories, protein 7.6g, carbohydrate 155.3g, fat 21.5g, saturated fat 7g, fibre 3.2g, sugar 117g, salt 1.24g

Everyone loves cherry pie – especially when it's a cherry crumble pie. These little pies are gorgeous hot, served with a spoonful of clotted cream.

Cherry crumble pies

FOR THE PASTRY AND TOPPING
200g/8oz plain flour
50g/2oz hazelnuts, ground
140g/5oz cold butter, cubed
50g/2oz caster sugar

FOR THE FILLING
3 rounded tbsp raspberry or bramble jelly
500g/1lb 2oz cherries, stoned
50g/2oz hazelnuts, roughly chopped
2 tbsp demerara sugar

Takes 1 hour • Serves 12

1 Preheat oven to 190°C/fan 170°C/gas 5. Tip the flour, hazelnuts and butter into a food processor, then whiz to fine crumbs. Add the sugar, then mix briefly. Remove 3 rounded tablespoons of the mixture and set aside. Add 1–2 tablespoons cold water to the processor, then pulse to a dough. Knead briefly, then wrap in cling film and chill for 20 minutes.
2 Roll out the dough and stamp out rounds using a 10–12cm cutter, re-rolling the trimmings. Use to line 12 small tartlet tins or the 12 holes of a muffin tin.
3 Warm the jelly in a pan, then stir in the cherries. Spoon into the pastry cases. Stir the chopped hazelnuts and sugar into the reserved flour, hazelnut and butter mix, then sprinkle this over the cherries in their pastry cases. Bake for 25–30 minutes until lightly browned. Cool for 10 minutes, then turn out, loosening the edges of the pies with the tip of a knife.

• Per pie 257 kcalories, protein 3g, carbohydrate 29g, fat 15g, saturated fat 7g, fibre 1g, sugar 16g, salt 0.19g

Good old apple pie – you can't beat it. This one is mildly spiced with cardamom but, if you'd rather, you could use a pinch of ground cinnamon, nutmeg or mixed spice instead.

Spiced apple pie

1.5kg/3lb 5oz eating apples (Braeburns are ideal), peeled and thickly sliced
squeeze of lemon juice
pinch of ground cardamom
2 tbsp flour, plus extra for rolling
25g/1oz golden caster sugar, plus extra for dusting
500g pack shortcrust pastry
2 tbsp milk
whipped cream, ice cream or custard, to serve

Takes about 2 hours • Serves 6–8

1 Preheat oven to 220°C/fan 200°C/gas 7. Toss the apples with the lemon juice, then dab dry with kitchen paper. Sprinkle with the cardamom, flour and sugar, then toss well.
2 Cut away a third of the pastry. Dust a work surface with flour, then roll out the larger piece to the thickness of a £1 coin. Use to line a metal pie dish. Roll out the smaller piece for the lid.
3 Pile apples inside and paint around the rim of the pastry with milk. Top with the lid. Trim the edge, then crimp around the edges to seal, using your index finger and thumb.
4 Slash the top, brush with the milk, then dust with sugar. Bake for 20 minutes, then reduce oven to 190°C/fan 170°C/gas 5 and cook for 50 minutes more or until the pastry is golden and crisp. Serve warm or cold with whipped cream, ice cream or custard.

• Per serving (6) 522 kcalories, protein 5g, carbohydrate 76g, fat 24g, saturated fat 11g, fibre 6g, added sugar 6g, salt 0.36g

This updated version of the original apple recipe couldn't be simpler
– you don't even need a rolling pin.

Tarte Tatin with brandy cream

50g/2oz butter
50g/2oz golden caster sugar
½ tsp ground cinnamon
6 medium Cox's or similar apples,
peeled, quartered and cored
375g pack fresh ready-rolled
puff pastry

FOR THE BRANDY CREAM
200ml pot crème fraîche
2 tbsp icing sugar
1 tbsp brandy or calvados

Takes 45–55 minutes • Serves 4

1 Preheat oven to 220°C/fan 200°C/
gas 7. Melt the butter in a 20cm tarte tatin tin or
ovenproof frying pan with an ovenproof handle
over a medium heat, then stir in the sugar and
cook until starting to caramelize. Stir in the
cinnamon. Add the apples then cook for
10 minutes, stirring every so often. The apple
juices will ooze out at first but will soon thicken
and make a sauce. Remove from the heat.
2 Prick the pastry all over with a fork. Lay it over
the apples. Trim away to fit the top of the pan,
then tuck the pastry snugly around the apples,
and down the inside of the tin.
3 Bake for 20–30 minutes until golden. Leave
to settle for 5 minutes, then run a knife round
the edge to loosen. Turn out on to a plate to
serve, pastry-side down.
4 For the brandy cream, mix the crème fraîche
with the sugar and brandy or calvados, and
serve alongside the tart.

• Per serving 761kcalories, protein 8g, carbohydrate
77g, fat 48g, saturated fat 15g, fibre 3g, added sugar
21g, salt 1.12g

This towering beauty makes the perfect sweet centrepiece to a summer buffet or a great winter dish, as a lighter option for Christmas pudding. Keep it in the fridge until ready to serve.

Raspberry and coconut trifle cake

FOR THE CAKE
200g/8oz butter, softened
50g/2oz desiccated coconut, soaked
for 1 hour then squeezed dry
200g/8oz caster sugar
200g/8oz self-raising flour
1 tsp baking powder
4 eggs
1 tbsp milk
2 tbsp coconut cream

FOR THE LAYERS AND TOPPING
1 tbsp cornflour
4 tbsp icing sugar
600ml ready-made custard
4 tbsp Malibu (or white rum)
zest and juice of 1 lime
300g raspberries
370g jar raspberry jam
142ml pot double cream
fresh coconut, grated

Takes about 1 hour 15 minutes, plus soaking and chilling • Serves 12

1 Preheat oven to 180°C/fan 160°C/gas 4. Butter and line a deep 20cm loose-bottomed tin. Beat the cake ingredients until smooth, then bake for 40–45 minutes until golden and risen.
2 Blend the cornflour, 1 tablespoon of the icing sugar and the remaining coconut cream. Heat the custard, then whisk in the coconut mix until boiling and thickened. Leave to cool, covered with cling film to prevent a skin forming.
3 Mix the rum, lime zest and juice and 2 tablespoons of the icing sugar. Cut the cake into three layers. Sprinkle with the rum mix.
4 Line the cleaned tin with cling film. Crush 100g of the raspberries and mix with jam. Fold in 100g of whole raspberries. Assemble the cake sandwiching with raspberry mix and custard. Cover and chill for at least 4 hours.
5 To serve, top with cream whipped with the final tablespoon of icing sugar then scatter with whole raspberries and grated coconut.

• Per serving 557 kcalories, protein 6.5g, carbohydrate 68.9g, fat 29.4g, saturated fat 17.9g, fibre 1.8g, sugar 53g, salt 0.72g

The plums and meringue can be prepared ahead, making this
a perfect dessert for a late-summer dinner party.

Brown sugar meringues with red wine plums

1 tsp cornflour
1 tsp wine vinegar
1 tsp vanilla extract
3 egg whites
100g/4oz caster sugar
50g/2oz light muscovado sugar

FOR THE PLUMS
200ml/7fl oz red wine
85g/3oz light muscovado sugar
1 cinnamon stick
9 large ripe plums, halved and stoned
400g/14oz crème fraîche

Takes 2 hours • Serves 6

1 Preheat oven to 140°C/fan 120°C/ gas 1. Line a baking sheet with baking parchment. Blend the cornflour, vinegar and vanilla extract into a paste. In a another bowl, whisk the egg whites until stiff and glossy. Add the sugar and cornflour paste gradually. Whisk back to firm peaks each time.

2 Spoon six meringue heaps on to the baking sheet then shape into nests using the back of a spoon. Bake for 1 hour, then turn off the oven and leave to cool.

3 Put the wine, sugar and cinnamon stick in a medium pan and bring to the boil. Add the plums and poach for 4–5 minutes until tender. Remove the plums, peel off the skins, then set aside. Boil the juice for 5 minutes to create a thick syrup, then cool.

4 Spoon crème fraîche and plums on to each meringue and drizzle over the syrup.

• Per serving 467 kcalories, protein 4g, carbohydrate 53g, fat 27g, saturated fat 17g, fibre 2g, sugar 52g, salt 0.16g

An updated version of a classic pear puddings. The poaching syrup can be frozen and used to poach other fruits.

Spiced poached pears in chocolate sauce

FOR THE PEARS
750g/1lb 10oz golden caster sugar
1 cinnamon stick
2 strips lemon zest
1 star anise
1 vanilla pod, split lengthways
5 cloves
a knob of fresh root ginger, peeled and sliced
4 ripe pears, peeled

FOR THE CHOCOLATE SAUCE
200g/8oz good-quality dark chocolate, chopped
142ml double cream
150ml/¼pint full-fat milk
a pinch of ground cinnamon

vanilla ice cream, to serve

Takes 1 hour • Serves 4

1 In a pan big enough to hold the pears snugly, tip in the sugar, zest and spices. Half-fill the pan with water; bring to the boil. Simmer for 10 minutes to infuse, drop in the pears, cover and gently poach for about 30 minutes until soft. Turn off the heat and set aside. The pears can be poached up to 2 days ahead and kept in the poaching syrup in the fridge.
2 To make the chocolate sauce, tip the chocolate into a heatproof bowl. Bring the cream, milk and cinnamon to the boil, and pour over the chocolate. Stir until the chocolate has melted. To serve, drain the pears and, holding them by the stem, dip them in the chocolate sauce to cover completely. Serve each pear with a generous scoop of vanilla ice cream.

• Per serving 642 kcalories, protein 6g, carbohydrate 66g, fat 41g, saturated fat 22g, fibre 6g, sugar 58g, salt 0.08g

Raspberries, rose, orange and pistachio are Middle-Eastern flavours that come together in this pretty trifle. If you do use Turkish delight, serve what's left with coffee or mint tea after dinner.

Raspberry and rose trifles

2 cubes rose Turkish delight (optional)
500g pot good-quality fresh vanilla custard
½ x 350g shop-bought Madeira loaf
300g pack raspberries
juice of 1 orange
200ml pot crème fraîche (use reduced-fat, if you like)
a handful of pistachio nuts, roughly chopped

Takes 10 minutes, plus chilling
Serves 6

1 If you don't want to add the Turkish delight, move on to step 2. Snip the Turkish delight into pieces with kitchen scissors into a large bowl and add a few tablespoons of water. Microwave on High for 1 minute, stirring after 30 seconds, or until dissolved and smooth. Tip in the custard and stir together.
2 Break the cake into rough chunks and divide among six sundae dishes or serving glasses. Mix half of the raspberries with the orange juice and crush gently with a fork to break up the fruit slightly. Spoon over the cake layer. Cover with the custard, then leave to cool in the fridge for at least 30 minutes. Can be made up to 1 day ahead.
3 To serve, top the trifles with a dollop of crème fraîche, the remaining raspberries and a sprinkling of pistachios.

• Per serving 380 kcalories, protein 6g, carbohydrate 35g, fat 26g, saturated fat 15g, fibre 2g, sugar 24g, salt 0.41g

Swirls of cherries give this sublime cheesecake a fruity summer flavour – perfect for a sunset dinner party.

Cherry swirl cheesecake

FOR THE BASE
50g/2oz butter, melted, plus extra for greasing
140g/5oz shortbread biscuits, finely crushed
1 tbsp golden syrup

FOR THE FILLING
350g/12oz cherries, 200g of them stoned
200g/8oz caster sugar
500g/1lb 2oz medium-fat soft cheese
1 tbsp cornflour
2 eggs
1 tsp vanilla extract
zest of 1 orange
200ml tub crème fraîche
icing sugar, for dusting

Takes 1 hour, plus cooling • Serves 8

1 Preheat oven to 160°C/fan 140°C/gas 3. Butter and line a loose-based 20cm cake tin. Mix the butter and shortbread crumbs. Tip into the tin and smooth with a spoon. Bake for 10 minutes, then cool. Reduce the oven temperature to 150°C/fan 130°C/gas 2.

2 To make the filling, tip the stoned cherries into a processor with 85g of the sugar. Once smooth, tip into a pan and bring to the boil. Simmer for 5–6 minutes, stirring, until it forms a thick syrup then leave to cool.

3 Rinse out the processor. Tip in the remaining sugar, cheese, cornflour, eggs, vanilla extract, zest and half the crème fraîche. Blend until smooth. Spoon half on to the biscuit base, cover with half the cherry syrup, then top with the remaining cheese mix. Swirl syrup through the top layer of cheese using a skewer. Bake for 45 minutes. Turn off the oven and leave to cool for 30 minutes then remove to cool further. Decorate with whole cherries and icing sugar.

• Per serving 506 kcalories, protein 10g, carbohydrate 51g, fat 31g, saturated fat 19g, fibre 1g, sugar 41g, salt 0.3g

There's no hanging about with this quick and easy trifle,
enriched with mascarpone instead of the usual cream.

Raspberry mascarpone trifle

10–12 sponge fingers
300g/10oz fresh or frozen raspberries
juice of 2 oranges
1 tbsp cassis
250g pot mascarpone
425g can or 500ml pot custard

Takes 10 minutes • Serves 6

1 Break up the sponge fingers into a
large bowl and scatter over most of the
raspberries, orange juice and cassis.
2 Beat the mascarpone with the custard
until smooth. Spoon the custard mix over the
fruit and sponge, scatter over the remaining
raspberries, and serve.

• Per serving 311 kcalories, protein 4.7g, carbohydrate
24.7g, fat 21.8, saturated fat 13.5, fibre 1.4g, sugar
19.5g, salt 0.25g

These cute cakes make the perfect finish to a special dinner, plus you can bake the sponge up to 2 days ahead. Serve with a small glass of kirsch on the side.

Little Black Forest cakes

25g/1oz butter, melted and cooled, plus extra for greasing
5 eggs
140g/5oz caster sugar
25g/1oz cocoa powder
100g/4oz self-raising flour
284ml pot double cream
4 tbsp kirsch, plus extra to serve
250g/9oz cherries, 6 left whole, rest stoned
25g/1oz plain chocolate, grated

Takes about 40 minutes • Serves 6

1 Preheat oven to 190°C/fan 170°C/gas 5. Butter and line a 30x35cm (or thereabouts) Swiss roll tin. Using electric beaters, whisk the eggs and sugar until thick and pale and the mix leaves a trail when the beaters are lifted. This will take about 5–6 minutes.
2 Sift the cocoa and flour over the mixture, then fold in using a large metal spoon. Drizzle over the melted butter, then fold in. Pour the mix into the tin and tilt the tin to level it off. Bake for 10–12 minutes until springy.
3 Turn out on to a wire rack to cool. Peel off the paper. Whip the cream until it holds its shape.
4 Cut 12 rounds from the cake using a 7–8cm cutter or a glass, then sprinkle with kirsch. Top six sponge rounds each with cream and stoned cherries, then another circle of sponge. Finish with the remaining cream, a sprinkling of grated chocolate and a whole cherry.

• Per cake 570 kcalories, protein 9g, carbohydrate 47g, fat 37g, saturated fat 19g, fibre 1g, sugar 33g, salt 0.45g

Friends and family will demolish this fresh and fruity cheesecake in no time!

Pineapple and passion fruit cheesecake

FOR THE BASE
10 digestive biscuits, crushed finely
6 ginger nut biscuits, crushed finely
85g/3oz unsalted butter, melted

FOR THE FILLING
2 × 300g tubs full-fat soft cheese
3 large eggs, beaten
142ml pot double cream
140g/5oz caster sugar
zest of 3 limes

FOR THE TOPPING
284ml pot double cream
1 tbsp icing sugar
1 medium, ripe pineapple, cored and thinly sliced
3 ripe passion fruit, halved

Takes 1 hour 20 minutes, plus coolin
Serves 8–10

1 Preheat oven to 160°C/fan 140°C/gas 3. Tip all the biscuits into a bowl and mix in the melted butter. Spoon the crumbs into the base of a 23cm springform tin and press down well. Bake for 10–15 minutes until lightly browned, then cool.

2 Put all of the filling ingredients in a large bowl and beat until smooth. Pour on to the cooled biscuit base and return to the oven for 50 minutes–1 hour until the filling is just set and starting to brown. Leave the cheesecake to cool in the oven with the door slightly open, then chill in the fridge. If the top has cracked, it doesn't matter as it will be hidden by the fruit. Remove from the tin to a serving plate.

3 To make the topping, whip the cream and icing sugar until thickened. Spread over the top of the cheesecake, then pile the pineapple on top. Scoop out the pulp and seeds of the passion fruit and scatter over the top to finish.

• Per serving (8) 799 kcalories, protein 10g, carbohydrate 52g, fat 63g, saturated fat 36g, fibre 2g, sugar 38g, salt 1.23g

Alcohol sets more softly than other liquids, so for the required wobble these jellies should to be very well chilled. Make them a day ahead, then whip them out of the fridge just before serving.

Strawberry and prosecco jellies

200g/8oz caster sugar
450g/1lb strawberries, hulled and quartered, plus 12 extra for decoration, quartered
6 sheets leaf gelatine
750ml bottle prosecco

Takes 20 minutes, plus chilling • Serves 6

1 Put the sugar and 150ml of water in a large pan and heat gently until the sugar has dissolved. Add the strawberries, boil, then bubble for 5 minutes without stirring, until the fruit has softened and the liquid is red, fragrant and syrupy.
2 Strain the hot syrup through a sieve into a large jug (be careful not to push the strawberries through the sieve as the jelly will become cloudy), then leave to cool for a few minutes. Discard the strawberries. While the syrup cools, soak the gelatine in cold water. Wring the gelatine sheets out with your hands, then stir into the warm syrup until completely melted.
3 Divide the extra strawberries among six 200–250ml champagne flutes or stemmed glasses. Open the prosecco, mix it briefly with the strawberry syrup, then pour over the strawberries. Chill overnight, then serve.

• Per serving 296 kcalories, protein 6g, carbohydrate 55g, fat none, saturated fat none, fibre 1g, sugar 55g, salt 0.08g

This cake needs to be assembled just before serving, though the meringues can be made up to a month ahead and frozen.

Praline meringue cake with strawberries

FOR THE MERINGUE
175g/6oz whole almonds, toasted
200g/8oz golden caster sugar
200g/8oz light muscovado sugar
6 egg whites
1 tbsp cornflour
2 tsp white wine vinegar

TO ASSEMBLE
1kg/2lb 3oz strawberries, hulled and halved, or quartered if large
50g/2oz icing sugar, plus extra for dusting
568ml pot double cream

Takes 1½ hours, plus cooling
Serves 12

1 Preheat oven to 140°C/fan 120°C/gas 1. Line 2 baking sheets with baking paper. Whiz two-thirds of the almonds in a processor until finely chopped. Roughly chop the rest.
2 Stir the sugars together. Whisk the whites until stiff, then add the sugar, cornflour and vinegar in three batches, whisking until stiff each time. Whisk until the mix is really stiff. Fold in the finely chopped nuts and most of the roughly chopped nuts, then spread in 20cm circles on the baking sheets. Scatter with the remaining nuts. Bake for 1 hour. Turn off the oven. Leave to cool for at least 1 hour.
3 Whiz 600g of strawberries in a processor then add 2 tablespoons of icing sugar. Sieve the remaining icing sugar into the cream. Whip then swirl through the sauce.
4 Sandwich and top meringues with the strawberry cream. Top with the remaining strawberries, dust with icing sugar then serve.

• Per serving 533 kcalories, protein 7g, carbohydrate 51g, fat 35g, saturated fat 15g, fibre 2g, sugar 50g, salt 0.16g

These gorgeous glassfuls are perfect after a spicy meal. Assemble them just before serving otherwise the meringue will start to dissolve.

Mango and cardamom syllabub

4 large mangoes, peeled and stoned,
2 finely chopped
10 green cardamom pods,
seeds only
finely grated zest and juice of 2 limes
85g/3oz icing sugar
4 tbsp brandy
568ml pot double cream
4 meringue nests, lightly crushed
mint sprigs, to decorate

Takes 25 minutes • Serves 8

1 Put the flesh of the two peeled and stoned mangoes in a food processor, and blend to a purée. Stir in almost all the finely chopped flesh of the other two mangoes, then spoon into the base of eight glasses.
2 Grind the cardamom seeds to a powder, then put in a bowl with the lime zest and juice, icing sugar and brandy. Stir well, then tip in the cream and whip until it holds its shape. Fold in the crushed meringues.
3 Spoon the cream mixture on top of the mango purée, then spoon the remaining chopped mango on top. This can be made 1 hour ahead. Serve decorated with mint sprigs.

• Per serving 537 kcalories, protein 3g, carbohydrate 43g, fat 39g, saturated fat 22g, fibre 4g, sugar 42g, salt 0.07g

Winter's answer to the strawberry pavlova – this is a great buffet or dinner-party dessert. Add the topping just before you serve.

Pecan toffee meringue with mulled pears

FOR THE MULLED PEARS
600ml/1 pint mulled wine
(ready-made from a bottle)
6 small ripe pears, peeled,
quartered and cored
50g/2oz golden caster sugar

**FOR THE PECAN MERINGUE
AND FILLING**
200g/8oz golden caster sugar
1½ tsp cornflour
4 egg whites
1½ tsp wine vinegar
50g/2oz pecan nuts, roughly
chopped
500g pot Greek yogurt
4 tbsp dulche de leche
extra toasted pecan nuts (optional)

Takes 1 hour 40 minutes, plus cooling
Serves 8–10

1 Put the wine, pears and sugar in a pan, and simmer for 10 minutes. Preheat oven to 160°C/fan 140°C/gas 3. Line a baking sheet with baking paper. Stir the sugar and cornflour together. Whisk the egg whites until stiff, then whisk in the sugar mixture, a tablespoon at a time, until thick and glossy.

2 Fold in the vinegar and half the nuts, then pile onto the paper and spread out to a 25cm circle, with a dip in the middle. Scatter with chopped pecans then put in oven, turning it down to 150°C/fan 130°C/gas 2. Bake for 1 hour, turn off the oven and leave to cool inside for 1 hour.

3 Remove the pears from the juice and simmer it until glossy. Return the pears to the juice and leave to cool. Combine the yogurt and dulche de leche. To serve, top the meringue with filling and pears. Scatter with more pecans, if using. Hand round the syrup for guests to spoon over, if they like.

• Per serving (8) 390 kcalories, protein 9g, carbohydrate 51g, fat 14g, saturated fat 5g, fibre 2g, sugar 50g, salt 0.26g

Whisked sponges are famously low in fat – especially if you fill them with yogurt instead of cream.

Mango and passion fruit roll

3 eggs
85g/3oz golden caster sugar, plus
1 tbsp
85g/3oz plain flour, sifted
1 tsp baking powder, sifted
1 tsp vanilla extract

FOR THE FILLING
1 tbsp golden caster sugar
pulp from 2 large, ripe passion fruit
2 mangoes, peeled and cut into
small chunks
250g pack frozen raspberries,
defrosted
200g tub 2% Greek yogurt or very
low-fat fromage frais

Takes about 40 minutes, plus cooling
Serves 10

1 Preheat oven to 200°C/fan 180°C/gas 6. Grease and line a 30x24cm Swiss-roll tin with baking parchment. Put the eggs and 85g sugar into a large bowl and beat with electric beaters until thick and light, about 5 minutes. Fold in the flour and baking powder, then the vanilla extract. Tip into the tin, tilt it to level, then bake for 12–15 minutes until golden and just springy. Turn out on to another sheet of paper, dusted with 1 tablespoon caster sugar. Roll the paper up inside the sponge, then leave to cool.
2 To make the filling, fold the sugar, passion fruit and one-third of the mango and raspberries into the yogurt. Unroll the sponge, spread with the filling, roll up again and serve with the rest of the fruit on the side. The roulade can be filled and rolled up to 2 hours before serving and kept in the fridge.

• Per serving 153 kcalories, protein 5g, carbohydrate 28g, fat 3g, saturated fat 1g, fibre 2g, sugar 21g, salt 0.26g

This is a fantastic cake to serve as a dessert or at teatime over the festive season. It can be made ahead too.

Dark chocolate and cranberry roulade

1 tbsp plain flour, for dusting
50g/2oz self-raising flour
1 tsp baking powder
25g/1oz good-quality cocoa powder, sifted
50g/2oz ground almonds
5 eggs
100g/4oz caster sugar, plus extra for turning the cake out

FOR THE FILLING
2 × 250g cartons mascarpone
zest of 1 orange
300g jar good-quality cranberry sauce (or use homemade)

FOR THE FROSTING
175g/6oz unsalted butter, softened
50g/2oz icing sugar, sifted
200g/8oz good-quality plain chocolate, melted and cooled

TO DECORATE
cranberries and bay leaves (optional)
icing sugar, to dust

Takes 1 hour 10 minutes, plus cooling
Serves 10

1 Preheat the oven to 190°C/fan 170°C/ gas 5. Butter and line a 30x40cm Swiss roll tin, then butter the parchment, dust with plain flour, tiping out any excess.
2 Mix the self-raising flour, baking powder, cocoa and almonds. Beat the eggs and sugar for 7–10 minutes until pale and thick. Fold in the dry ingredients. Pour into the tin then bake for 12–15 minutes or until firm.
3 Cool for 1 minute, then turn out on to a sheet of sugared baking parchment. Remove the lining paper and roll up the sponge, rolling the parchment inside.
4 Beat the mascarpone with the zest. Unroll the sponge, remove the paper. Spread with mascarpone and cranberry sauce. Roll up again.
5 For the frosting, beat the butter and icing sugar until pale then stir in the chocolate. Leave to firm for 20 minutes then spread over the roulade. Decorate then chill until ready to serve.

• Per serving 691 kcalories, protein 9g, carbohydrate 48g, fat 52g, saturated fat 29g, fibre 2g, sugar 26g, salt 0.45g

Adding lime juice along with the passion fruit sets the cream in these possets a little firmer than usual, so they transport really well.

Passion fruit pots with coconut stars

125g/4½oz caster sugar
568ml pot double cream and 284ml pot double cream
8 ripe passion fruit (look for wrinkly ones)
2 tbsp lime juice

FOR THE SHORTBREAD
100g/4oz butter, softened
140g/5oz plain flour, plus a little extra for dusting
85g/3oz ground rice
85g/3oz desiccated coconut
2 egg yolks
¼ tsp vanilla extract
200g/8oz caster sugar
plus 1 tbsp extra, to decorate

Takes 40 minutes, plus chilling
Serves 10

1 Combine the sugar and all the cream in a heavy-bottomed pan. Heat gently, stirring, until the sugar has dissolved, then boil fiercely for 3 minutes, stirring. Take off heat. Sieve the pulp from seven of the passion fruit, then stir the juice and the lime juice into the cream. It will thicken. Cool for 10 minutes, then pour into 10 small pots or cups. Cool, then cover with cling film. Chill for 3 hours or overnight to set.
2 Preheat oven to 180°C/fan 160°C/gas 4. Stir the butter, flour, ground rice, 50g of the coconut, egg yolks, vanilla extract and sugar into a dough. Roll out on a floured surface and stamp out stars. Spread over baking sheets lined with baking parchment, sprinkle with the remaining coconut, dust with extra sugar, then bake for 8–10 minutes until golden. Cool.
3 To serve, scoop the pulp from the remaining passion fruit and drizzle a little over each pot. Arrange the crunchy coconut stars on the side.

• Per serving 793 kcalories, protein 5g, carbohydrate 59.8g, fat 60.9g, saturated fat 35.8g, fibre 2g, sugar 41.4g, salt 0.23g

This is a great dessert to bring to a party because it needs to be served cold and can be happily made a day ahead.

Orange chocolate tart

500g pack dessert pastry

FOR THE FILLING
5 eggs
200g/8oz caster sugar
juice and zest of 4 oranges
juice of 1 lemon
142ml pot double cream
140g/5oz plain chocolate, chopped
and melted

FOR THE CARAMELIZED ORANGE
SALAD
2 oranges, peeled and zest finely
shredded
200g/8oz caster sugar

Takes 2 hours, plus chilling
Serves 10

1 Preheat oven to 200°C/fan 180°C/gas 6. On a floured surface, roll the pastry to line a 23cm loose-bottomed tart tin, leaving an overhang. Line with baking paper, fill with baking beans, and bake on a baking sheet for 20 minutes. Remove the beans and cook for 10 minutes more until golden. Cool. Reduce the oven temperature to 150°C/fan 130°C/gas 2.
2 Whisk the eggs, sugar, orange and lemon juice, zest and cream in a large jug. Once pastry is cool, trim overhang, then brush inside with chocolate. Chill, then repeat. Pour in the custard. Bake for 45–50 minutes until just set, then cool.
3 For the salad, segment the oranges, catching any juices. Put the zest in a pan of cold water, boil, then strain and set aside. Melt the sugar in a pan with a little water, then boil to an amber caramel. Tip in the zest, orange segments and juice. Swirl everything around, then cool. Serve with the tart.

• Per serving 602 kcals, protein 7.6g, carbohydrate 79.5g, fat 30.4g, saturated fat 12.7g, fibre 1.8g, sugar 60.4g, salt 0.38g

Plums, chocolate and hazelnuts – this is a perfect cake for an autumn celebration. Enjoy a slice with your mid-morning coffee or serve it warm for dessert.

Plum, hazelnut and chocolate cake

175g/6oz butter, softened, plus extra for greasing
500g/1lb 2oz plums
175g/6oz light muscovado sugar
175g/6oz self-raising flour
175g/6oz hazelnuts, ground
3 eggs
1 tsp baking powder
50g/2oz plain chocolate (70% cocoa solids), chopped
2 tbsp hazelnuts
2 tbsp redcurrant, damson or plum jelly

Takes 1 hour, plus cooling • Serves 8

1 Preheat oven to 180°C/fan 160°C/gas 4. Butter and line the base of a 20cm round cake tin. Halve and stone 4 plums, set aside for later, then roughly chop the remainder.
2 Put the sugar, butter, flour, ground hazelnuts, eggs and baking powder into a large bowl and beat for 1–2 minutes until smooth and light. Stir in the chopped plums and chocolate, then tip into the prepared cake tin and smooth the top.
3 Arrange the halved plums over the top of the mixture, pressing them down lightly, then scatter over the hazelnuts. Bake for 40–50 minutes until the top is golden and the cake feels firm to the touch. Cool in the tin for 10 minutes, then turn out, remove the paper and cool on a wire rack. Heat the jelly, then brush over the top of the cake before serving.

• Per serving 581 kcalories, protein 9g, carbohydrate 51g, fat 39g, saturated fat 15g, fibre 4g, sugar 33g, salt 0.83g

Summer birthdays deserve a special summery cake like this one, layered with fruit and a creamy filling.

Raspberry layer cake

FOR THE CAKE
200g/8oz caster sugar
200g/8oz butter, softened
4 eggs, beaten
200g/8oz self-raising flour
1 tsp baking powder
icing sugar, to dust

FOR THE SYRUP
85g/3oz caster sugar
50ml/2fl oz almond liqueur

FOR THE FILLING
284ml pot double cream
250g tub mascarpone
3 tbsp caster sugar
150g punnet raspberries

Takes 50 minutes, plus chilling overnight • Serves 8

1 Preheat oven to 190°C/fan 170°C/gas 5. Butter and line 2 x 20cm sandwich tins. In a large bowl, beat together all the cake ingredients to a smooth, soft mixture. Divide between the two tins, smoothing the tops, then bake for 25–30 minutes or until golden and the cake springs back when gently pressed. Turn out the cakes on to a wire rack to cool.
2 For the syrup, heat the sugar, 2 tablespoons water and the liqueur together until the sugar has dissolved. Cool a little. Use a large serrated knife to cut each cake in half. Brush the syrup over all four pieces of cake with a pastry brush.
3 For the filling, whip the cream until it forms soft peaks. Beat the mascarpone and caster sugar in a large bowl to loosen, then fold in the cream. Layer the fruit, cream and sponges, finishing with a layer of sponge. Press lightly, then wrap tightly in cling film and chill overnight.

• Per serving 819 kcalories, protein 8g, carbohydrate 68g, fat 58g, saturated fat 33g, fibre 2g, sugar 50g, salt 1.02g

Using polenta and fresh strawberries makes these little cakes especially light and fragrant.

Strawberry and polenta cupcakes

140g/5oz unsalted butter, softened
140g/5oz golden caster sugar
grated zest of ½ lemon
85g/3oz polenta
3 eggs, beaten
140g/5oz plain flour
1 tsp baking powder
1 tbsp milk
140g/5oz strawberries, hulled and chopped

TO DECORATE
3 strawberries, hulled and roughly chopped, plus 6 halved
juice of 1 lemon
140g/5oz icing sugar, sifted

Takes 35 minutes, plus cooling
Makes 12

1 Line a 12-hole muffin tin with paper cases and preheat oven to 180°C/fan 160°C/gas 4. Beat together the butter, sugar and lemon zest until pale. Beat in the polenta followed by the eggs, a little at a time.
2 Sift in the flour and baking powder, then fold in quickly with a large metal spoon. Stir in the milk, then fold in the chopped strawberries. Spoon into paper cases; bake for 20 minutes or until golden and risen. Cool on a wire rack before peeling the cases from the cakes.
3 For the icing, place the chopped strawberries in a bowl with 1 teaspoon of the lemon juice and mash to a pulp. Sieve, then add to the sugar with a little lemon juice to turn it pink. Stir in more lemon juice, drop by drop, to make a thick but flowing icing. Dip each cake into the icing, then top with a strawberry half. Leave to set, then serve.

• Per cake 271 kcalories, protein 4g, carbohydrate 40g, fat 12g, saturated fat 7g, fibre 1g, sugar 26g, salt 0.19g

No one will be able to resist a slice of this. If you prefer lemon cake, use lemons instead of oranges and lemon curd instead of orange curd.

Orange drizzle cake

FOR THE SPONGE
200g/8oz soft butter, plus extra for greasing
200g/8oz self-raising flour, sifted
1 tsp baking powder
200g/8oz golden caster sugar
4 eggs
2 tbsp milk
zest of 2 oranges

FOR THE DRIZZLE
100g/4oz white sugar cubes
zest of 1 orange, plus 2 tbsp juice

FOR THE FILLING
100ml pot crème fraîche
6 tbsp orange curd

Takes 40 minutes • Serves 8

1 Preheat oven to 180°C/fan 160°C/gas 4. Grease and bottom-line 2 x 20cm round sandwich tins with baking paper, then lightly grease the paper. Add all the sponge ingredients to a large bowl, then beat everything together until smooth. Divide the mix between the cake tins, then bake for 20–25 minutes until risen and golden. When cool enough to handle, remove the cakes from the tins, then leave to cool completely on a wire rack.
2 For the drizzle, roughly crush the sugar cubes with the orange juice and zest until they absorb the juice and become slushy.
3 For the filling, whip the crème fraîche until stiff. Spread over one of the sponges, then spread the other with orange curd and sandwich the two together. Spoon over the drizzle, let it soak in, then serve.

• Per serving 548 kcalories, protein 7g, carbohydrate 66g, fat 30g, saturated fat 18g, fibre 1g, sugar 45g, salt 0.95g

You'll be amazed at how professional this cake looks once it's glazed.
Serve with crème fraîche flavoured with a little clementine zest.

Sticky clementine cake

12 seedless clementines
450g/1lb golden caster sugar
200g/8oz butter, softened, plus a
little extra for greasing
zest of 1 lemon
3 eggs, separated
300g/10oz ground almonds
100g/4oz fine polenta
150g pot natural yogurt

Takes 1 hour 50 minutes, plus cooling
Serves 10

1 Preheat oven to 180°C/fan 160°C/gas 4. Thinly slice 5 clementines, discarding the ends. In a small pan, melt 250g of the sugar in 300ml boiling water, then simmer. Add the clementine slices, cover and cook for 20 minutes until tender. Grease and bottom-line a 25cm springform tin.
2 Lift the slices from the syrup and arrange in the tin. Zest the remaining 7 clementines, then squeeze the juice from 4 and add it to the pan. Boil for 10 minutes to a thick syrup.
3 Beat the remaining sugar, butter, lemon and clementine zests until pale. Beat in the egg yolks one by one. Peel the 3 remaining zested clementines; whiz the flesh in a processor until pulpy. Stir into the batter with the almonds, polenta and yogurt. Whisk the egg whites to stiff, then fold in. Spoon into the tin; bake for 1 hour until a skewer inserted in the centre comes out clean. Cool in the tin.
4 To serve, turn the cake out on to a serving plate and top with sticky syrup.

• Per serving 603 kcalories, protein 10.9g, carbohydrate 62.4g, fat 36.2g, saturated fat 12.6g, fibre 3.1g, sugar 54.8g, salt 0.43g

Apricots and raspberries are really good partners and are especially good baked into this soft vanilla cake topped with cinnamon crumble.

Apricot and raspberry buckle

175g/6oz self-raising flour, plus 2
rounded tbsp
200g/8oz softened butter
2 tbsp demerara sugar
2 tsp ground cinnamon
175g/6oz caster sugar
3 eggs
2 tsp vanilla extract
6 apricots, stoned and sliced
200g/8oz raspberries, fresh or frozen
cream or ice cream, to serve

Takes 1 hour 10 minutes, plus cooling
Serves 8

1 Preheat oven to 180°C/fan 160°C/gas 4. Butter and line the base of a 23cm square tin. For the crumble mix, put the 2 tablespoons of flour and 25g of the butter in a bowl with the demerara sugar and cinnamon. Rub between your fingers until it resembles damp breadcrumbs.
2 Tip the remaining flour and butter, and the caster sugar, eggs and vanilla extract in to a bowl, then beat until well combined. Lightly fold in half the apricots and raspberries, then spoon the mix into the prepared tin.
3 Scatter over the remaining fruit, then sprinkle with the crumble mix. Bake for 45–50 minutes until light golden, then cool for 10 minutes and remove from the tin. Cut into squares and serve warm with cream or ice cream for dessert, or cold for tea.

• Per serving 437 kcalories, protein 6g, carbohydrate 53g, fat 24g, saturated fat 14g, fibre 2g, sugar 33g, salt 0.72g

Impress your friends and family with this fabulous celebration cake. You could swap the berries for whatever soft fruit is in season, then change the jelly in the filling for a matching jam.

Blackberry and almond meringue cake

FOR THE CAKE
200g/8oz butter, softened
200g/8oz golden caster sugar
200g/8oz self-raising flour
50g/2oz ground almonds
2 eggs and 2 egg yolks, beaten
2 tbsp milk (you may need a splash more)
150g punnet blackberries

FOR THE MERINGUE
2 egg whites
100g/4oz golden caster sugar, plus a sprinkle
2 tbsp flaked almonds

FOR THE FILLING
200ml/7fl oz double cream, lightly whipped
4 tbsp bramble jelly

Takes 1½hours, plus cooling • Serves 8

1 Line the base of 2 x 20cm round non-stick sandwich tins with baking parchment. Preheat oven to 160°C/fan 140C/gas 3.
2 Put all the cake ingredients (except the blackberries) in a bowl, then beat until creamy and well mixed. Stir in 100g of the blackberries, plus a little more milk to loosen, if needed. Spoon into sandwich tins and level the tops.
3 To make the meringue, quickly whisk the egg whites in a clean bowl, gradually adding the sugar until really thick and glossy. Lightly spread on to one of the cake mixtures, then sprinkle with almonds and a little sugar. Bake both cakes for 40 minutes, then remove the cake without the meringue top. Bake the meringue-topped cake for 30 minutes more until a skewer inserted in the centre comes out clean. Cool on a wire rack. Once cold, peel away the parchment.
4 Spread the cream over the plain cake. Spoon over the bramble jelly. Sandwich with the meringue cake and decorate with blackberries.

• Per serving 668 kcalories, protein 9g, carbohydrate 67g, fat 43g, saturated fat 22g, fibre 2g, sugar 48g, salt 0.75g

This indulgent cake is perfect for tea in the garden. Be careful when you're checking if it's cooked – don't mistake melted white chocolate for raw cake mix.

White chocolate and cherry loaf

FOR THE CAKE
200g/8oz butter, softened
200g/8oz golden caster sugar
4 eggs, beaten
2 tsp vanilla extract
200g/8oz self-raising flour,
plus extra for dusting
375g/13oz fresh cherries, pitted
175g/6oz white chocolate, chopped
into small chunks

FOR THE WHITE CHOCOLATE FROSTING
100g/4oz white chocolate, broken
into small pieces
140g/5oz half-fat mascarpone, room
temperature
white chocolate curls, to decorate

Takes 1½ hours, plus cooling
Serves 12

1 Preheat oven to 180°C/fan 160°C/gas 4. Line a 1kg-loaf tin with baking parchment, bringing the paper up higher than the sides. Beat the butter and sugar until fluffy, then add the eggs, a little at a time, along with the vanilla extract. Fold in the flour until smooth.
2 Dust the cherries in a little flour, then stir half the fruit and all the chocolate into the cake mixture. Spoon into the tin, then scatter the remainder on top, pressing in lightly. Bake for 1¼ hours until a skewer inserted into the centre comes out clean. Cool in the tin for a few minutes, then on a wire rack.
3 For the frosting, melt the chocolate in a bowl over a pan of simmering water. Stir in 1 tablespoon of the mascarpone, then mix in the rest. Spread over the cake and finish with white chocolate curls.

• Per serving 485 kcalories, protein 7g, carbohydrate 53g, fat 29g, saturated fat 17g, fibre 1g, sugar 39g, salt 0.63g

If you fancy this cake but don't have a ring mould, follow the recipe using a 20cm round tin. Increase the cooking time to 50 mins - 1hour.

Peach, redcurrant and soured cream ring

FOR THE TOPPING
3 ripe peaches, skinned, halved and stoned
5 tbsp peach conserve
100g/4oz fresh redcurrants

FOR THE CAKE
250g/9oz self-raising flour
1 tsp baking powder
175g/6oz butter, softened
175g/6oz golden caster sugar
2 eggs, beaten
1 tsp vanilla extract
4 tbsp milk
170ml pot soured cream

Takes 55 minutes, plus cooling
Serves 6

1 To make the topping, cut a small cross at the base of each peach, plunge them into boiling water for a few seconds, and then straight into cold. Peel away the skins, then halve and stone. Preheat oven to 190°C/fan 170°C/gas 5 and butter a non-stick 23cm ring tin. Arrange the peaches, cut-side up, in the base of the tin, then spoon in the peach conserve and scatter over the redcurrants.

2 To make the cake, beat together the flour, baking powder, butter, sugar, eggs, vanilla extract and milk until well mixed, then stir in the soured cream. Spoon the mixture into the cake tin, then level the surface.

3 Bake for 35–40 minutes until the cake is well risen, golden, and springs back when lightly pressed. Cool for a few minutes, then carefully turn out on to a plate. You can serve warm with cream as a dessert or cold as a cake for tea.

• Per serving 605 kcalories, protein 8g, carbohydrate 78g, fat 32g, saturated fat 19g, fibre 3g, sugar 46g, salt 1.20g

Peaches and cream – a classic combination that's made even tastier in cake form. The peach sponge base will take a little longer to cook, and needs to be handled delicately.

Upside-down peaches and cream cake

FOR THE SPONGE
200g/8oz soft butter, plus extra for greasing
200g/8oz self-raising flour
1 tsp baking powder
200g/8oz golden caster sugar
4 eggs
2 tbsp milk

FOR THE PEACH TOPPING
3 ripe peaches, cut into eighths
85g/3oz light muscovado sugar

FOR THE FILLING
2 × 116g tubs clotted cream
2 tbsp golden caster sugar
½ tsp vanilla extract

Takes 55 minutes, plus cooling
Serves 8

1 Preheat oven to 180°C/fan 160°C/gas 4. Grease and bottom-line 2 x 20cm round non-stick sandwich tins with baking parchment, then lightly grease the paper. Add all the sponge ingredients to a large bowl, then beat everything together until smooth.
2 Toss the peaches with the sugar, then arrange in a single layer in one of the tins. Tip half the cake mix over the peaches and the other half into the second tin. Bake for 20–25 minutes until cooked and golden – the tin containing the peaches may take 5–10 minutes longer than the other. Leave to cool on a wire rack while you make the filling.
3 Whisk the clotted cream with the sugar and vanilla extract until stiff. Spread this over the plain sponge, then carefully place on the peach-topped sponge.

• Per serving 658 kcalories, protein 7g, carbohydrate 64g, fat 43g, saturated fat 26g, fibre 1g, sugar 45g, salt 0.94g

If you're cooking this recipe in winter, when fresh gooseberries are impossible to find, then frozen berries work just as well.

Gooseberry gems

200g/8oz self-raising flour
1 tsp baking powder
200g/8oz golden caster sugar
3 eggs
150g pot natural yogurt
4 tbsp elderflower cordial
175g/6oz butter, melted and cooled
icing sugar, for dusting

FOR THE FOOL
350g/12oz gooseberries, topped and tailed (or use frozen)
50g/2oz golden caster sugar
1 tbsp elderflower cordial
200g pot crème fraîche

Takes 30 minutes, plus cooling
Makes 12

1 Preheat oven to 200°C/fan 180°C/gas 6. Line a 12-hole muffin tray with paper cases. Mix the dry ingredients together in a large bowl. Beat the eggs, yogurt, elderflower cordial and melted butter with a pinch of salt, then stir into the dry ingredients. Spoon into the cases, bake for 18–20 minutes until risen and golden, then cool on a wire rack.

2 Gently cook the gooseberries with sugar in a pan for 10 minutes until the berries have collapsed a little. Taste, add more sugar if you like, then stir in the cordial and cool. Fold into the crème fraîche.

3 To serve, cut a section from the top of each cake using a small, serrated knife or, if that's too fiddly, simply cut off the top and cut it in half, like a butterfly cake. Spoon fool into each cake, top with the piece that you cut away, then dust with a little icing sugar.

• Per cake 370 kcalories, protein 5g, carbohydrate 43g, fat 21g, saturated fat 13g, fibre 1g, sugar 29g, salt 0.61g

Here's a versatile cake–perfect for picnics, eaten as a dessert or enjoyed as an indulgent bite with a cup of tea.

Apricot and blueberry crumble cake

300g/10oz apricots, skinned, halved and stoned (or use a drained 410g can instead)
200g/8oz butter, softened
200g/8oz golden caster sugar
200g/8oz self-raising flour
1 tsp baking powder
3 eggs, beaten
2 tbsp milk
150g pot vanilla yogurt
200g/8oz punnet blueberries

FOR THE CRUMBLE
25g/1oz butter
3 heaped tbsp self-raising flour
3 tbsp demerara sugar
1 tsp ground cinnamon

Takes about 1 hour, plus cooling
Serves 12

1 If using fresh apricots, cut a small cross at the base of each fruit, plunge into boiling water for a few seconds, then straight into cold. Peel away the skins, then halve and stone. Line a tray bake tin (21 x 30cm) with baking parchment and preheat oven to 180°C/fan 160°C/gas 4. Beat the butter, sugar, flour, baking powder, eggs and milk together until creamy. Spoon into the tin, level the top, then bake for 25 minutes until almost set.
2 Meanwhile, make the crumble by rubbing all the ingredients together.
3 After 25 minutes in the oven, take out the cake and quickly spoon over the yogurt, scatter over the fruit, then top with the crumble. Return to the oven for 15–20 minutes until a skewer comes out clean when inserted in the centre of the cake. Serve warm as a pudding, or cooled and cut into squares for tea.

• Per serving 443 kcalories, protein 8g, carbohydrate 66g, fat 18g, saturated fat 11g, fibre 2g, sugar 29g, salt 0.84g

A fruit cake for those who like theirs light, spicy and moist. Full of Christmassy flavours, the cranberry tartness of the topping complements the spicy sweetness of the cake.

Posh spice cake

FOR THE CAKE
85g/3oz self-raising flour
140g/5oz wholemeal plain flour
1 tsp baking powder
175g/6oz golden caster sugar
finely grated zest of 1 small orange
¼ teaspoon ground cardamon
½ tsp cinnamon
½ tsp mixed spice
¼ tsp nutmeg
140g/5oz butter, cut in pieces
100g/4oz pecan nuts, half chopped,
half left whole
85g/3oz raisins
85g/3oz sultanas
85g/3oz dried cranberries
1 egg
100ml/4fl oz milk

FOR THE CRANBERRY TOPPING
85g/3oz cranberries
25g/1oz golden caster sugar

Takes 2 hours, plus cooling
Serves 12

1 Butter and line the base of a deep, 18cm round loose-bottomed cake tin. Preheat oven to 160°C/fan 140°C/gas 3. Mix the flours, baking powder, sugar, zest and spices.
2 Rub the butter into the mix until it looks like coarse crumbs. Stir in the chopped pecans, raisins, sultanas and cranberries. Beat the egg and milk together and stir into the mixture. Spoon into the tin, level the top, scatter over the remaining pecans and bake for 90 minutes, lowering the heat to 150°C/fan 130°C/gas 2 after 45 minutes.
3 Toss the cranberries in the sugar. After the cake has cooked for 90 minutes, spoon over the cranberries. Bake for 15–20 minutes until the cranberries are sticky and a skewer inserted into the cake comes out clean.
4 Cool in the tin. The cake is best kept overnight before slicing, to allow the flavours to mellow.

• Per serving 346 kcalories, protein 4.4g, carbohydrate 47.2g, fat 16.8g, saturated fat 7g, fibre 2.4g, sugar 33.4g, salt 0.42g

This cake is as light as a soufflé and matches pears with their perfect partner – chocolate. Try it with dollops of cream or crème fraîche.

Flourless chocolate and pear cake

85g/3oz butter, plus 1 tbsp for greasing
85g/3oz golden caster sugar, plus extra for tin
85g/3oz chocolate, broken into pieces
1 tbsp brandy
3 eggs, separated
85g/3oz hazelnuts, toasted and ground in a food processor
4 very ripe pears, peeled, cored and halved
icing sugar, for dusting

Takes 1 hour, plus cooling • Serves 8

1 Grease a 25cm round loose-bottomed tin with butter, line the bottom with baking parchment and grease. Swirl some sugar around the tin to coat it, tipping out any excess.
2 Preheat oven to 180°C/fan 160°C/gas 4. Melt the chocolate and butter in a bowl over a pan of simmering water, take off the heat, stir in the brandy and let cool. Whisk the egg yolks with the sugar in a large bowl until pale and thick.
3 With clean beaters, whisk the egg whites to soft peaks. Stir a spoonful into the chocolate mix, then fold in the rest in two stages. Fold in the hazelnuts. Spoon into the tin, level and add the pears. Bake for 40 minutes. Cool in the tin slightly before releasing then cooling completely on a wire rack. Dust with icing sugar to serve.

• Per serving 334 kcalories, protein 5g, carbohydrate 28g, fat 23g, saturated fat 9g, fibre 2g, sugar 28g, salt 0.28g

Index

Picture and recipe credits

BBC *Good Food* magazine and BBC Books would like to thank the following people for providing photos. While every effort has been made to trace and acknowledge all photographers, we should like to apologize should there be any errors or omissions.

Marie-Louise Avery p43; Peter Cassidy p71, p109, p143; Jean Cazals p85, p87, p107, p125, p135, p175; Will Heap p69, p139, p141; Tim Macpherson p167; Gareth Morgans p29, p33, p35, p45, p49, p121, p127; David Munns p31, p41, p73, p75, p93, p179, p191, p195, p203; Noel Murphy p37; Myles New p17, p67, p131, p163, p187; Elisabeth Parsons p15, p19, p25, p51, p65, p78, p105, p114, p149, p169, p171, p173, p177, p180, p182, p189, p197, p199, p201, p207; Craig Robertson p6, p96, p99, p101, p103; Roger Stowell p11, p13, p53, p77, p89, p111, p117, p147, p155, p161, p165, p185; Debbie Treloar p112, p137; Simon Walton p47, p59, p63, p123, p129, p157; Philip Webb p21, p23, p39, p55, p60, p83, p91, p95, p119, p133, p144, p159, p192, p205, p208, p210; Simon Wheeler p151; Kate Whitaker p27, p57

All the recipes in this book were created by the editorial team at *Good Food* and by regular contributors to the magazine.